THE SPIRITUAL CORPORATE

From Chaos to Clarity—The New
DIY Code for Professional Breakthrough

Paromita Banerjee Sarkar

Made with ♥ on the Notion Press Platform

www.notionpress.com

Table of Contents

Foreword

✦ *"In a world that glorifies hustle,*

pausing to heal is the bravest act of all.

*Success means nothing if your soul is weary."** ✦

— **Paromita Banerjee Sarkar**

Founder, Timeless Soul Healings

Look around you—truly look. The world as we knew it is evolving at a pace we've never experienced before. Technology, culture, communication, and expectations—everything is shifting rapidly. We live in an age of constant movement, where innovation is celebrated, speed is worshipped, and the race for relevance never stops. This world is fiercely competitive, boundlessly creative, and—let's be honest—often brutally unforgiving.

What worked even a decade ago may no longer hold true. The strategies that elevated our predecessors, the leadership lessons they swore by, the balance they maintained between work and life—all of that is now being questioned, recalibrated, and in many cases, rendered obsolete. We're no longer living in an era where following a fixed path guarantees success. We're in an age of disruption, uncertainty, and transformation. So the question is not just "How do we keep up?" but **"How do we evolve?"**

If the playing field has changed, shouldn't our approach change too?

What if surviving this modern whirlwind isn't just about running faster, working harder, or outshining the competition? What if it's about **working smarter, living more consciously, and evolving from the inside out?** What if success today isn't about being the loudest voice in the room, but the most aligned one?

This book is born from that question.

It invites you to consider a different lens—**one that fuses the enduring wisdom of ancient philosophy with the boldness, creativity, and adaptability demanded by the modern world.** Think of it as a bridge between the past and the future. The meditative stillness of inner mastery walking hand-in-hand with the dynamic fire of external success. This is not about abandoning the hustle. It's about infusing the hustle with meaning. It's not about choosing between ambition and peace—it's about achieving both through conscious alignment.

In the chapters ahead, we will explore ideas and techniques that don't just help you cope, but teach you to **thrive in the midst of chaos.** You'll learn how to build a career that aligns with your soul, how to manage stress without sacrificing performance, and how to unlock new levels of clarity, confidence, and creativity.

Because the truth is—**we're not here just to survive changing times.**

We're here to rise above them.

To redefine what success looks like.

To thrive, with purpose.

Let the journey begin.

Chapter 1

The Corporate Stress Epidemic

🌐 The New Reality: Stress is the Silent Pandemic of the Corporate World

In the early 21st century, the corporate world underwent a seismic shift.

Technology promised freedom, automation pledged simplicity, and globalization expanded horizons.

And yet, hidden beneath these breakthroughs, another less visible phenomenon was spreading silently, relentlessly — **the epidemic of corporate stress.**

The past few years, especially post the **global pandemic,** have amplified what was already simmering.

Suddenly, dining tables became offices, bedrooms became conference rooms, and the fragile walls between personal life and professional identity **crumbled.**

The "always available" culture exploded.

Work hours blurred into personal time. Meetings piled upon meetings. Expectations skyrocketed, while human connection diminished.

Today, **stress in the workplace** isn't a rare occurrence.

It's a **daily companion** for millions across sectors — tech, finance, education, healthcare, hospitality, you name it.

"It's not just a bad week or a tough month anymore," said Ananya, a senior HR professional.

"It's a constant hum of exhaustion vibrating underneath everything we do."

We have accepted **chronic stress** as the price of ambition, the tax for success.

But at what cost?

📊 Alarming Numbers: Stress By The Data

- **76%** of employees experience stress daily (Gallup 2022).

- **44%** report severe burnout symptoms at work.

- **1 million** people miss work every day due to stress (American Institute of Stress).

- WHO projects that **stress-related disorders will be the second leading cause of disability** worldwide by 2030.

Behind each statistic is a human story — dreams deferred, health shattered, relationships strained.

Corporate stress is no longer an individual issue.

It is a **collective, systemic crisis.**

🧠 The Neuroscience of Workplace Stress: Your Brain Under Siege

When you encounter a stressful event — a missed deadline, a toxic boss, a job layoff rumor — your brain's **amygdala** immediately springs into action.

It signals the release of cortisol and adrenaline, preparing your body for survival.

But corporate life today is a **never-ending series of micro-threats**: emails, targets, restructuring, comparison, promotions.

There is no real break. Your body stays trapped in **chronic fight-or-flight**.

Chronic cortisol surges lead to:

- Shrinking of the **prefrontal cortex** (decision-making center)
- Overactivation of the **limbic system** (emotional regulation)
- Weakened **immune system** and increased inflammation
- Memory lapses, poor judgment, irritability

Imagine running a marathon...with no finish line.

That's what corporate employees are doing every day.

⬣ The Cost of Success: Emotional Bankruptcy

Many professionals, despite lucrative salaries, corner offices, and fancy titles, confess to feeling **emotionally bankrupt**.

Here's the emotional iceberg lurking under corporate suits:

- A CMO earning ₹60L+ yearly admits crying in his car before important meetings.
- A project manager on the verge of promotion secretly struggles with insomnia and chronic anxiety attacks.

- A senior tech engineer, exhausted by back-to-back sprints, cannot remember the last time she spent an evening without her laptop.

The pursuit of external success, when untethered from inner alignment, breeds emptiness.

🔒 Why Traditional Corporate Wellness Programs Fail

Corporates have tried to counter rising stress with a host of initiatives:

Zumba sessions, weekend yoga retreats, resilience webinars, desk meditation apps.

But why do these efforts often fall flat?

1. Superficial Solutions

Employees are offered fitness tips when what they truly need is **emotional healing**.

2. Lack of Personalization

Everyone's stress triggers are unique. One-size-fits-all workshops cannot solve deeply personal emotional wounds.

3. Short-Term Focus

Wellness initiatives are often **episodic events**, not integrated cultural shifts.

4. Ignorance of Emotional and Energetic Layers

True healing happens **beyond the rational mind**—it happens in the heart, the body, and the soul.

Ignoring these layers ensures the stress will return... sometimes even stronger.

♡ Real Stories: Stress Unmasked

Case Study 1: Rohan's Silent Breakdown

Rohan Kapoor was the quintessential successful CEO: articulate, visionary, tireless.

But behind his sharp suits and TED Talks, **he was falling apart.**

Sleepless nights. Random panic attacks. A deep, gnawing dread that wouldn't leave.

Meditation apps? Tried.

Pilates sessions? Completed.

Therapy? Briefly.

Nothing shifted — until he tried Emotional Freedom Technique (EFT).

Tapping gently on specific meridian points, Rohan found suppressed grief from childhood — a fear of not being enough.

Through persistent inner work, his panic attacks reduced by 80% within six months.

His blood pressure normalized.

He began to lead with authenticity, not fear.

Case Study 2: Aditi's Invisible Battle

Aditi Sharma, 34, had checked every success box:

- MBA from a top B-school
- Marketing head at an MNC
- A six-figure income

But inside, she felt invisible.

The chronic back pain, she realized during Hypnohealing sessions, was the body's cry for emotional attention.

By confronting her deeply buried fear of rejection (rooted in a turbulent adolescence), she experienced a **transformation not just in her health—but in her presence**.

Her voice grew stronger.

Her confidence bloomed.

She reclaimed joy at work she thought was lost forever.

Case Study 3: Vikram's Battle with Career Stagnation

After 12 years in IT consulting, Vikram felt trapped.

Each promotion cycle brought fresh disillusionment. Despite working 70+ hours a week, recognition always seemed elusive.

Through **NLP Future Pacing exercises** and **EFT Tapping** for impostor syndrome, Vikram realigned his subconscious scripts.

Six months later, he transitioned into a product head role in a dynamic start-up — and rediscovered his zest for innovation.

🧘 The Urgent Call for Holistic Healing in Corporates

Modern workplaces need to evolve from a **stress-driven culture** to a **soul-driven culture**.

Holistic practices are the bridge:

- **Energy Healing (EFT, Reiki, Chakra Clearing):** Dissolves blocked emotional energy.

- **Mindfulness & Meditation:** Trains the mind to respond, not react.

- **Past Life Regression & Shadow Work:** Unlocks hidden emotional patterns.

- **Tarot Life Coaching:** Provides intuitive guidance and clarity for career crossroads.

- **Hypnohealing:** Reprograms subconscious beliefs sabotaging growth.

Healing is not a "soft skill."

It's a **survival skill for the modern age**.

🚀 The Future of Workplaces: Spiritual Intelligence Meets Corporate Strategy

Progressive companies like Google, Sales force, and LinkedIn are already investing heavily in mindfulness, emotional intelligence, and resilience training.

Tomorrow's successful organizations will not just be data-driven.

They will be **soul-driven**.

Imagine workplaces where:

- Emotional check-ins matter as much as sales targets.

- Leadership development includes energy management.

- Career growth conversations focus on **alignment, not exhaustion**.

That is the future of sustainable success.

✵ Conclusion: Beyond Survival — Toward Soulful Success

The corporate stress epidemic is real—and growing.

But so is the collective yearning for **something more.**

For work that nourishes, not depletes.

For careers that expand our soul, not shrink it.

For success measured not just by profits, but by **peace of mind and joy of living.**

Holistic healing practices like EFT, NLP, Past Life Regression, Shadow Work, Hypnohealing, and Tarot Life Coaching are **not luxuries anymore.**

They are lifelines.

As we embark on this journey together, remember:

Healing yourself is the most revolutionary act you can perform in today's stressed-out corporate world.

Welcome to a new era.

An era where **success and soul** walk hand in hand.

Chapter 2

Spirituality & Success — The Missing Link

"The soul was never meant to chase deadlines.

It was meant to create, to connect, and to rise."

— Paromita Banerjee Sarkar

✧ Understanding Spirituality Beyond Religion

In corporate boardrooms and buzzing startups alike, **spirituality** often carries a cloud of misconception.

It's frequently equated with religion—rituals, worship, dogma.

But true **spirituality**, especially in the modern professional context, **transcends boundaries of religion**.

Spirituality is not about what you believe.

It's about **how you live, how you connect**, and **how aligned you are with your true self**.

In corporate life, spirituality shows up when:

- A leader inspires trust through authenticity.

- A team member steps into courage during uncertainty.
- A founder decides to prioritize people over profits.

It's about being **centered** amid chaos, **ethical** amid ambition, and **compassionate** amid competition.

✸ Quote

"Spirituality is not a belief system.

It's a way of being—true, whole, and awake."

🚀 How Spirituality Enhances Corporate Success

The most resilient, innovative, and successful professionals are not necessarily the most competitive—they are the most **aligned**.

When you are spiritually connected:

- You operate from **clarity, not confusion**.
- You make **decisions rooted in intuition**, not fear.
- You inspire **loyalty through authenticity**, not authority.

A groundbreaking **Harvard Business Review (2019)** study showed that executives who practiced mindfulness, compassion-based leadership, and deep inner reflection were:

- **40% more likely to build high-performing teams**
- **30% less likely to burn out**
- **25% more creative in problem-solving**

Companies like **Google, Sales force**, and **Apple** are living proof.

They have invested heavily in mindfulness spaces, gratitude practices, and emotional resilience training—not as a luxury, but as a **competitive advantage**.

✨ Quote

"Inner alignment breeds outer excellence."

🌍 Key Benefits of Spiritual Practices in the Workplace

Let's break it down practically:

Benefit	**Impact on Career**
Emotional Intelligence	Better teamwork, conflict resolution, leadership presence
Enhanced Decision-Making	Quicker, wiser choices in high-pressure moments
Work-Life Balance	Healthier employees = higher long-term productivity
Creativity and Innovation	Out-of-the-box solutions, agile mindset
Stress Resilience	Less absenteeism, higher focus, emotional agility

🌍 The Science Behind Spirituality and Success

🧘‍♂️ Neuroscience and Mindfulness

Thanks to pioneering researchers like **Dr. Richard Davidson** at the University of Wisconsin, we now know:

- Long-term meditators have **thicker prefrontal cortexes**—boosting focus and emotional regulation.
- Regular mindfulness shrinks the **amygdala** (the brain's fear center), reducing reactivity to stress.
- **Grey matter density increases** in regions linked to learning, memory, and emotional regulation.

Simply put, spirituality—practiced through mindfulness, meditation, or gratitude—**rewires the brain for success.**

✨ Quote

"Your greatest competitive edge is not in your resume.

It's in your nervous system."

🌀 Energy Science and Workplace Success

Beyond neuroscience, ancient wisdom systems reveal that **emotional blocks create energy blocks**.

Techniques like:

- **Chakra balancing**
- **Emotional Freedom Technique (EFT)**
- **Reiki**

help release these blockages—leading to **enhanced clarity, emotional stability, and creative flow.**

Incorporating even 5 minutes of daily energy work has been shown to reduce cortisol levels by **over 30%** (University of California Study, 2021).

🔥 Practical Spiritual Practices for Professionals

Morning Mindfulness Routine:

- **5 minutes** of focused breathing.

- **Gratitude journaling**: Write down 3 things you're grateful for.

- **Visualization**: Picture yourself flowing through your day with ease and success.

Energy Cleansing Techniques:

- **Breathwork before meetings**: Breathe in light, exhale stress.

- **Chakra realignment**: Visualize light flowing from your crown to your feet.

Grounding Exercises:

- **Nature Connection**: Barefoot walks, even for 2 minutes.

- **Stretching Breaks**: Move your body consciously to stay rooted.

Micro-Meditations:

- **2-minute silent breaks** between Zoom calls.

- **Visualization Reset**: Imagine a clear blue sky washing away mental clutter.

✺ Quote

"Stillness is not a luxury for high performers. It is their fuel."

💼 Real-Life Corporate Case Studies

Case Study 1: Vikram — The CFO Who Rewrote His Inner Story

Vikram Sharma was the Chief Financial Officer of a billion-dollar firm.

On paper, he was a success.

Behind closed doors, he battled crippling anxiety before board meetings, insomnia, and emotional numbness.

Introduced to **Mindfulness-Based Stress Reduction (MBSR)** by a colleague, Vikram committed to a 10-minute morning meditation.

Within 6 months:

- His anxiety attacks reduced by 70%.
- He reported making decisions with greater clarity and confidence.
- His team noticed his growing emotional presence—resulting in improved team morale and performance.

"I used to think spirituality was for monks. Today, it's my leadership secret weapon," Vikram smiles.

Case Study 2: Tara — From Corporate Burnout to Soulful Success

Tara Verma, a 32-year-old tech product manager, was driven, ambitious—and burned out.

An accidental introduction to **Tarot Coaching** and **Chakra Healing** opened new doors.

Through guided sessions, she realized her root chakra was blocked by survival fears stemming from childhood insecurity.

Working weekly on energy alignment, journaling, and micro-meditations, Tara transformed:

- She switched to a purpose-driven startup aligned with her values.
- Her health improved (migraines reduced).
- Her creative ideation sessions became legendary in her new company.

"Spirituality didn't make me less ambitious. It made me unstoppable—with peace," says Tara.

📑 Case Study 3: Amit — Techie's Journey to Authentic Leadership

Amit, a senior software architect, struggled with impostor syndrome despite awards and accolades.

Shadow Work exercises and Inner Child Healing unlocked old wounds of "not being good enough."

As he embraced daily affirmations and emotional tapping rituals:

- Amit began asserting his ideas confidently.
- He successfully pitched a product idea that became a flagship innovation.
- His sense of worth became intrinsic—not dependent on external validation.

"I no longer hustle for approval. I lead from my truth," Amit affirms.

🌟 Quote

"When you heal internally,
external success becomes inevitable."

🏢 How Companies Can Integrate Spirituality into Corporate Culture

Forward-thinking organizations are embracing **soulful success**:

Best Practices

- **Mindfulness Workshops**: Weekly group meditations.
- **Energy Healing Circles**: Chakra balancing sessions post-project closures.
- **Flexible Reflection Breaks**: 15-minute mental health check-ins.
- **Gratitude Walls**: Employees posting daily gratitude.
- **Vision Alignment Coaching**: Helping employees align personal values with corporate missions.

Companies like **Salesforce**, **LinkedIn**, and **Google** have already pioneered these models—with measurable improvements in retention, creativity, and employee satisfaction.

🌟 Quote

"When companies nurture souls,
they don't just grow profits. They grow legacies."

✻ Conclusion: Reclaiming Success With Soul

Spirituality is not anti-ambition.

It is **aligned ambition**.

When professionals root themselves in their higher consciousness:

- Stress doesn't break them.
- Pressure doesn't corrupt them.
- Success doesn't empty them.

Instead, they **expand**, **enrich**, and **elevate**—personally and professionally.

"Your soul is not the enemy of your ambition. It is its greatest ally."

Welcome to a new paradigm.

A world where **success is soulful**, and **work is a vehicle for awakening, not exhaustion.**

———•●•———

Chapter 3

Emotional Freedom Technique (EFT) for Stress & Confidence

The Inner Earthquake: Stress in the Professional World

Every morning, millions of professionals wake up with tight chests, racing thoughts, and the familiar hum of anxiety. Whether it's the dread of an upcoming presentation, office politics, an overwhelming workload, or the silent self-doubt that whispers "You're not good enough," the modern workplace is filled with triggers that drain emotional energy and erode confidence.

What if we told you there was a simple yet powerful tool to regulate this emotional chaos—something you could do in just a few minutes a day without needing any equipment, therapy sessions, or even a quiet room?

Enter: **Emotional Freedom Technique (EFT)**, also known as **Tapping**.

⚲ Understanding Emotional Freedom Technique (EFT)

EFT is a self-healing tool that blends the wisdom of **ancient acupressure** with the science of **modern psychology**. Developed initially by psychologist Dr. Roger Callahan and later simplified by Gary Craig, EFT targets energy meridians in the body—pathways through which life-force or "chi" flows.

It's based on the principle that **unresolved emotional issues create energetic disruptions**, which manifest as stress, anxiety, low confidence, or even physical pain. By tapping gently on specific meridian points while voicing affirmations, we're telling the body:

"You are safe. You are heard. Let's release this now."

◍ The Science Behind Why EFT Works

Multiple studies have supported EFT's effectiveness in reducing stress and reprogramming the brain's response to triggers.

⚖ Key Findings

- **Cortisol Reduction**: A landmark study published in *The Journal of Nervous and Mental Disease* found that a single session of EFT reduced cortisol levels (the body's stress hormone) by **up to 43%**.

- **Neuroplasticity**: According to research from Harvard Medical School, stimulating acupressure points calms the **amygdala**—the brain's fear center—reducing the fight-or-flight response.

- **Brainwave Shift**: EEG scans show increased **alpha and theta waves** during EFT, associated with deep relaxation, emotional release, and enhanced focus.

EFT is not a placebo. It's a tool for **emotional rewiring**.

✂️ Step-by-Step: How EFT Works

EFT involves tapping on nine meridian points while stating the emotional issue and repeating a self-acceptance phrase.

✋ Step 1: Identify the Core Issue

What are you feeling? Be honest.

"I feel anxious about my upcoming appraisal."

"I feel not good enough in meetings."

📊 Step 2: Rate the Intensity

On a scale from 0 to 10, how intense is the emotion?

🧘 Step 3: Craft the Set-Up Statement

"Even though I feel _____, I deeply and completely accept myself."

☝️ Step 4: Tap Through the Meridian Points

Point	Purpose
Karate Chop (Side of Hand)	Breaks resistance
Eyebrow	Releases frustration
Side of Eye	Eases resentment

Point	Purpose
Under Eye	Calms anxiety
Under Nose	Strengthens confidence
Chin	Grounds emotion
Collarbone	Settles the nervous system
Under Arm	Encourages self-acceptance
Top of Head	Brings clarity

Repeat your set-up phrase or let natural emotions surface as you tap.

✅ Step 5: Reassess

Check your intensity level again. Has it reduced? Tap again if needed with revised phrasing.

✳ Quote

"Tapping is like emotional acupuncture—

without the needles."

💼 Case Study 1: Rahul — Overcoming Public Speaking Anxiety

Rahul, a senior marketing manager at a reputed firm, was brilliant at strategy but panicked at the thought of speaking in meetings. Despite knowing his subject, his hands would tremble, voice shake, and he'd mentally blank out.

❀ EFT in Action

- Rahul began tapping 10 minutes every morning and just before key meetings.

- He used the phrase: *"Even though I fear sounding stupid, I choose to feel calm and confident."*

- He also tapped while visualizing himself confidently presenting.

⅋ Result

Within four weeks, Rahul gave a flawless presentation to a 200-member audience and received a standing ovation.

"It wasn't that the fear disappeared overnight. But now, it doesn't control me," he says.

◔ Case Study 2: Priya — Healing from Burnout

Priya, a financial analyst, was working 12-hour days under a demanding boss and relentless targets. She developed migraines, insomnia, and irritability. She considered quitting.

A friend introduced her to EFT.

✿ Her Practice

- Morning tapping: *"Even though I feel exhausted and overwhelmed, I choose to breathe and be kind to myself."*

- Post-work tapping to decompress.

⚘ Result

After six weeks, Priya reported:

- 50% improvement in sleep
- Reduction in daily headaches
- Renewed passion for her work

She also used EFT before difficult client calls to remain calm and composed.

💡 Real-World Application: EFT for Common Workplace Triggers

Let's explore how EFT can be applied to **real scenarios professionals face**:

Trigger	EFT Focus
Fear of feedback	"Even though I dread criticism, I choose to grow and feel safe."
Imposter Syndrome	"Even though I feel I don't belong, I choose to trust my abilities."
Toxic boss dynamics	"Even though I feel powerless, I choose to stand in my strength."
Fear of job loss	"Even though I feel anxious about my job, I choose to trust my future."

❋ Quote

"When you tap into your energy, you take your power back."

✏️ Case Study 3: Suresh — Rising Beyond Self-Doubt

Suresh was a talented IT professional, always appreciated but never promoted. He later admitted:

"I didn't apply. I thought I'd fail."

Years of internalized beliefs—*"I'm not leadership material"*—held him back. A coach introduced him to EFT.

❇️ Implementation

- Tapped daily with affirmations like:
  "Even though I feel undeserving, I choose to see my worth."

- Tapped before writing his promotion application.

🌱 Result

- Applied confidently
- Nailed the interview
- Promoted to Tech Lead within 3 months

He now uses EFT with his team to boost morale and address performance fears.

🏢 Organizational Adoption: EFT Goes Mainstream

Large corporates all over the world have integrated emotional wellness strategies including EFT.

Benefits include:

- Reduced absenteeism
- Increased collaboration

- Boosted innovation due to emotional regulation

Forward-thinking leaders recognize that **emotions drive performance**. And EFT offers a way to regulate emotions in real time.

✍ Try This: EFT Daily Workplace Practice (5 Minutes)

1. Find a quiet spot.

2. Identify what's bothering you.

3. Tap through the points while saying:

   - *"Even though I feel _____, I choose to feel calm and capable."*

4. Breathe deeply.

5. Reassess and repeat if needed.

This practice, done regularly, can reset your emotional baseline.

❈ Quote

*"Stress is not your enemy. Suppressed emotion is.
EFT helps you release it safely."*

⅁ Conclusion: Tapping Into a New You

Emotional Freedom Technique is more than a tool—it's a **gateway to inner peace, self-belief,** and **emotional agility** in a world that constantly demands more.

Whether you're a CEO, a team leader, or an entry-level analyst, **your emotional health is your leadership currency.**

By learning to tap, you'll not only release stress—you'll reclaim the parts of you that stress silenced.

So, the next time you feel stuck, overwhelmed, or insecure—pause.

Tap.

Breathe.

Your power has been within you all along. You just needed a way to unlock it.

Chapter 4

Past Life Regression – Healing Unseen Blocks

✵ *"Sometimes the answers to today's struggles lie buried in yesterday's lifetimes."*

🐚 Introduction: When the Past Clings to the Present

Have you ever felt irrational fear while speaking up in meetings?

Or found yourself repeating the same toxic patterns in professional relationships?

Perhaps you've done everything "right" in your career—but success seems just out of reach.

What if these barriers aren't rooted in your present life... but in your past ones?

Past Life Regression (PLR) is not just a spiritual curiosity—it's a **deep healing modality** that brings clarity and transformation by accessing memories stored deep in the subconscious.

ᚙ Understanding Past Life Regression (PLR)

PLR is a technique that uses **hypnosis or deep meditation** to tap into the subconscious mind and **recall experiences from past incarnations**. It is rooted in the belief that our soul journeys through many lifetimes, and unresolved traumas or lessons can leave imprints that carry into our present careers, behaviors, fears, and relationships.

PLR sessions can bring up:

- Emotional residue from unhealed lifetimes
- Patterns of guilt, shame, or fear
- Soul contracts and karmic relationships
- Hidden talents or insights from previous lives

It's not about fantasizing the past. It's about **understanding the past to break free in the present.**

🗐 The Science & Research Behind PLR

While PLR remains outside mainstream clinical psychology, a growing number of researchers have studied its therapeutic benefits.

❁ Key Research

1. **Dr. Ian Stevenson**, University of Virginia:

   Studied over 2,500 children who recalled past-life memories with verifiable historical accuracy.

2. **Dr. Jim Tucker**, successor to Stevenson:

   Documented children describing past lives with remarkable detail, later confirmed via records.

3. **Dr. Brian Weiss**, former Chairman of Psychiatry at Mount Sinai:

   After a patient spontaneously regressed to a past life, Weiss became a pioneer in PLR, citing thousands of successful regressions leading to healing.

4. **Cellular Memory Theory:**

   Suggests that trauma and memory can be stored in our cells, not just the brain—explaining phobias or behaviors without a present-life cause.

5. **Subconscious Reprogramming:**

   Hypnosis (used in PLR) allows access to the theta brainwave state—where subconscious beliefs can be altered for lasting transformation.

�֎ Quote

"Your soul remembers more than your mind ever could."

🔍 How PLR Helps in Corporate Success

Even in the professional realm, **past-life imprints influence present-day performance.**

- Recurring issues like:
- Imposter syndrome
- Fear of visibility or leadership
- Trust issues with colleagues
- Inexplicable stress before success may all stem from **soul wounds** carried across lifetimes.

🔄 Common Career Issues & their PLR Roots:

Career Block	Potential Past-Life Root
Fear of Public Speaking	Punishment or execution for expressing truth
Fear of Success	Betrayal after achieving power or wealth
Overworking/ Burnout	Past vows of servitude or self-sacrifice
Trust Issues at Work	Past betrayal by a close partner or team
Feeling Undeserving	Past karma of misuse of power or privilege

🧘‍♀️ How PLR Sessions Work

A Past Life Regression session is a guided journey, typically led by a trained therapist or coach.

🔄 4-Step PLR Process

1. **Induction & Deep Relaxation**

   You are guided into a relaxed, theta-brainwave state through breathwork, visualization, or hypnosis.

2. **Journey Into the Past**

   Through questions or imagery, you access past-life scenes. You may see visuals, feel sensations, or "know" impressions intuitively.

3. **Processing & Release**

   You revisit key moments to understand emotions and release stored trauma or beliefs.

4. **Integration & Application**

   The therapist helps link past-life lessons to present-life patterns—and rewire limiting beliefs into empowering ones.

✨ Quote

"Healing doesn't always start with logic—
it often begins with remembering."

💼 Case Study 1: Rajveer – A CEO's Fear of Leadership

Despite his accolades and successful ventures, **Rajveer**, a 42-year-old CEO of a fintech company, struggled to lead decisively. He avoided confrontation and was plagued with self-doubt before major decisions.

📖 His Regression

Under hypnosis, Rajveer recalled a lifetime as a respected military commander during an ancient war. A strategic error cost many lives, and he was publicly disgraced.

In this lifetime, he subconsciously feared making leadership decisions out of guilt and trauma.

✨ Outcome

- After processing and releasing that guilt, Rajveer felt lighter, more centered.
- He began trusting his instincts and made bold decisions—including a successful merger that doubled company valuation.

"I didn't know I was still carrying the weight of a decision made centuries ago," he said.

🤝 Case Study 2: Workplace Conflict & Karmic Ties

Meera, an HR manager, and **Arjun**, a senior VP, had constant friction—clashing over policies, deadlines, and communication styles. No amount of coaching helped.

⑥ PLR Sessions (Separate)

Both underwent individual regression sessions.

Meera saw a lifetime as a village head betrayed by a trusted merchant. Arjun saw himself as that merchant—driven by greed but filled with regret.

✨ Outcome

Understanding this karmic loop brought compassion. Both engaged in a forgiveness ritual during coaching.

They now co-lead a leadership wellness program in their firm.

"Once we understood the soul history, the present made sense," said Meera.

🌐 Case Study 3: Anand – A Scientist's Intuitive Breakthrough

Dr. Anand, a researcher in green tech, hit a creative block for months. Meditation didn't help. He volunteered for a PLR session out of curiosity.

🔍 His Journey

He regressed into a lifetime in ancient Greece, as a philosopher experimenting with wind turbines. He remembered design sketches and concepts.

Days later, Anand had a breakthrough—connecting ancient wind channeling with modern renewable tech.

✨ Result

His team filed a patent on a new turbine prototype inspired by ancient principles.

Using PLR as a Self-Coaching Tool

While guided sessions are ideal, professionals can try self-guided regression through:

- Deep meditation
- Audio journeys by trusted PLR therapists
- Journaling post-meditation impressions
- Creating a "soul map" linking current challenges with intuitive past-life clues

Organizational Adoption of PLR

Though still emerging, some progressive organizations now explore **PLR as part of employee well-being programs.**

How Companies Can Integrate PLR:

1. **Wellness Retreats**

   Include PLR sessions alongside mindfulness, yoga, and emotional freedom techniques.

2. Coaching Circles

Certified regression coaches facilitate personal growth circles for emotional release.

3. Conflict Resolution

Pairing regression therapy with coaching for persistent interpersonal dynamics.

4. Leadership Development

Help high-potential employees explore karmic patterns around visibility, power, and responsibility.

❉ Quote

"You are not stuck. You are repeating.
PLR shows you what you're repeating and how to stop."

❉ Closing Thoughts: The Power of Remembering

Most corporate training focuses on the mind.

But true transformation begins in the soul.

Past Life Regression invites professionals to look beyond LinkedIn profiles, degrees, and resumes—and into the soul's journey.

It helps explain:

- Why some fears feel "irrational"
- Why you keep hitting the same wall
- Why success scares you more than failure

And best of all, it **liberates** you from unconscious patterns.

"You can't heal what you don't understand. PLR gives you the map—and the mirror."

So, the next time your career hits a strange block, ask not just "What am I doing wrong?"

Ask instead:

"What am I still carrying that no longer belongs to me?"

Your soul knows.

Let it guide you

 Chapter 5

Shadow Work Healing – Embracing Your Hidden Self

"Until you make the unconscious conscious, it will direct your life and you will call it fate."

— Carl Jung

Introduction: The Self Behind the Suit

Every day in the corporate world, professionals show up in polished shoes, carrying confident resumes, and hiding... shadows.

Behind high-performing teams and smiling Zoom calls often lie:

- The fear of being found out as a "fraud"
- The dread of failure that stalls big dreams
- The simmering resentment toward colleagues
- The suppressed anxiety of not being "good enough"

This emotional turbulence doesn't come from nowhere.

Much of it stems from the **shadow self**—the part of us we don't want to see.

Shadow Work is about **turning the mirror inward**, not to judge or shame ourselves, but to understand, heal, and **integrate the hidden parts** that quietly sabotage our growth.

🎯 What is the Shadow Self?

Carl Jung, the Swiss psychiatrist, coined the term **"shadow"** to describe the unconscious aspects of the personality we deny, suppress, or reject—usually because we believe they're undesirable, shameful, or socially unacceptable.

In a corporate context, the shadow might show up as:

- Unexplained jealousy of a colleague's success
- Harsh self-criticism after minor mistakes
- People-pleasing to avoid conflict
- Avoidance of leadership roles due to fear of scrutiny

These behaviors are **not flaws**. They are unintegrated parts of ourselves screaming for acknowledgment.

✺ How are Shadows formed?

The shadow self begins to take shape early in childhood, as we gradually learn which emotions, behaviors, and traits are welcomed—and which are not—by our families, schools, and the society around us. In our natural desire to belong and be accepted, we begin to hide or reject parts of ourselves that seem to invite disapproval. These disowned aspects don't disappear; instead, they retreat into the unconscious, slowly forming what Carl Jung called the "shadow"—a repository of suppressed feelings, desires, and qualities.

- **Social and Cultural Conditioning:** From a young age, we are molded by societal expectations about what is "right," "wrong," "strong," or "weak." Cultural messages can deeply influence how we express ourselves. For instance, boys may be conditioned to believe that showing emotion—especially through tears—is a sign of weakness. As a result, sadness or vulnerability gets pushed into the shadow, leading to emotional numbness or hidden grief later in life.

- **Family and Upbringing:** Our immediate family environment plays a pivotal role in shaping what we accept or reject within ourselves. If a child is repeatedly told to "keep quiet" or "stop being so dramatic," they may begin to suppress their natural enthusiasm or voice. Over time, this suppression can lead to a shadow aspect of unexpressed creativity, joy, or self-expression.

- **Personal Life Experiences:** Significant or painful events also contribute to the development of the shadow. A child who faces ridicule or bullying may internalize shame or fear, creating a hidden part of themselves that feels unsafe, unworthy, or hesitant to engage with others. This buried pain can later manifest as low self-confidence, avoidance of conflict, or difficulty trusting others.

🧠 The Science Behind Shadow Work

1. Neuroscience & Emotional Suppression

Studies from Stanford and UCLA show that **suppressing emotions activates the amygdala—the** brain's fear center—causing the body to stay in a state of low-grade stress. Over time, this impacts decision-making, memory, and focus.

2.   Psychological Impact

A study in *Psychological Science* revealed that individuals who regularly suppress emotions experience:

- Increased stress hormone levels
- Reduced resilience in high-pressure situations
- Higher likelihood of burnout and depressive symptoms

3. In the Workplace

Unacknowledged emotional wounds show up as:

Symptom	Rooted Shadow Trait
Avoiding leadership	Fear of responsibility or failure
Overworking	Deep fear of inadequacy
Perfectionism	Childhood belief of needing to "earn love"
People-pleasing	Fear of abandonment or rejection
Micromanaging	Fear of losing control

❂ Quote

"You can't outrun your shadow in the boardroom.
You can only bring it into the light."

✺ How Shadow Work Helps Professionals

Modern workplaces reward productivity—but **true performance stems from emotional clarity and inner alignment.**

Shadow Work is not therapy. It's **self-leadership**—a deep journey into the subconscious to remove emotional roadblocks and reclaim buried power.

✷ Benefits

- Improved communication and teamwork
- Greater confidence and resilience
- Freedom from unconscious self-sabotage
- Heightened emotional intelligence
- More authentic leadership presence

⬛ Common Corporate Challenges Shadow Work Can Resolve

Challenge	Shadow Root
Fear of speaking up	Shame from past invalidation
Inability to handle feedback	Fear of rejection
Avoiding promotions	Deep belief of not being capable
Constant burnout	Internalized guilt or martyrdom
Conflict with authority	Resentment from past control dynamics

⚇ The 5-Step Shadow Work Model for Professionals

Step 1: Identify the Trigger

Notice the moments that spark intense emotions—especially if the reaction seems disproportionate.

✿ *Example*: You feel angry when your teammate is praised. Pause. Ask yourself: "What am I really reacting to?"

Step 2: Name & Accept the Emotion

Instead of saying "I shouldn't feel this way," practice non-judgment.

⚇ *Affirmation*: "I feel jealous. That's okay. This is information, not condemnation."

Step 3: Self-Inquiry & Journaling

Reflect with questions like:

- When did I first feel this emotion?
- What part of me is feeling unseen or unworthy?
- What belief might be hiding underneath this reaction?

Step 4: Inner Dialogue

Imagine a safe space where you meet your "shadow self"—the part holding the suppressed emotion.

⚇ Ask

- "What are you afraid of?"
- "What do you need from me?"
- "How can I support you?"

Step 5: Integrate with Compassion

Bring the shadow into your conscious identity. Acknowledge its origin, and **reframe the belief**.

🌱 *New Belief*: "I can be confident and vulnerable. I am worthy even when I'm not perfect."

✳️ Quote

> *"Your triggers are not flaws—they are portals to transformation."*

👦💼 Case Study 1: Meena – From Fear of Authority to Poised Leadership

Meena, a capable project manager, avoided eye contact with executives, stumbled during presentations, and rarely spoke up in boardroom discussions.

⚙️ Shadow Root

During journaling, Meena recalled a strict father and school principal who often belittled her opinions as a child.

😊 Integration

- Practiced daily affirmations of worthiness.

- Wrote letters to her inner child acknowledging her pain.

- Visualized her younger self being celebrated for speaking up.

🦋 Result

Within three months, Meena led a cross-functional team presentation and was later promoted to Associate Director.

"I didn't need another degree. I needed to stop hiding from myself," she said.

Case Study 2: Amit – From Micromanagement to Empowerment

Amit, a Sales Director, had high turnover on his team. He frequently over-checked work, second-guessed decisions, and clashed with colleagues.

Shadow Root

Amit had built a business years ago that failed due to a partner's negligence. He internalized the belief: "If I don't control everything, I will be betrayed again."

Integration

- Journaled about that failure and forgave his past self.

- Created "trust rituals" with team members—weekly check-ins focused on appreciation.

- Practiced stepping back consciously from control urges.

Result

His team thrived, sales improved, and Amit said:

"Shadow Work taught me that trust starts with me."

Shadow Work & Emotional Intelligence

Integrating your shadow increases:

Skill	Benefit
Self-awareness	Recognize when ego or fear is speaking
Self-regulation	Pause before reacting to triggers
Empathy	See others beyond your projections
Leadership authenticity	Show up grounded and whole

▦ Corporate Integration of Shadow Work

Forward-thinking companies like **Google, SAP, and Adobe** are investing in **Emotional Intelligence (EQ)** training—which now often includes:

- Self-awareness assessments
- Reflective journaling
- Mindfulness and breathwork
- Shadow exploration exercises

🚀 How Organizations Can Apply It:

1. **Self-Awareness Workshops**

   Encourage safe spaces where employees identify emotional triggers and limiting beliefs.

2. **Leadership Circles**

   Executives reflect on personal narratives and rewrite internal scripts.

3. **Shadow Coaching Pods**

   Facilitated small groups to explore unconscious patterns and practice emotional regulation.

✵ Quote

> *"When leaders embrace their shadows,*
> *they become the light others can follow."*

🌈 Final Thoughts: Wholeness Is the New Power

Shadow Work isn't about fixing you. It's about **accepting the parts of you that you've ignored**—the scared inner child, the jealous competitor, the wounded achiever—and learning to lead with **wholeness, not perfection.**

Because the truth is:

- No promotion can silence self-doubt if the root is never healed.
- No corporate title will fill a void created by unacknowledged shame.
- And no salary can replace the joy of feeling truly **seen by yourself.**

Shadow Work is not the easiest journey. But it is the most liberating one.

You don't have to be perfect to be powerful.

You have to be real. And that starts within.

———•◆•———

 Chapter 6

Hypnohealing for Deep Mental Reprogramming

"The mind is everything. What you think, you become."

— *Buddha*

Introduction: The Unseen Script of the Subconscious

In the boardrooms of multinational corporations and the quiet cubicles of startups alike, a silent force shapes every decision, every reaction, and every ambition: the subconscious mind.

This hidden realm doesn't operate with logic or planning. It functions on **beliefs**—many of which were implanted in childhood or during emotionally intense moments. Some of these beliefs propel us forward. Others act like invisible anchors, keeping us stuck in fear, self-doubt, or underachievement, no matter how talented we are on paper.

Enter **Hypnohealing**—a practice that merges the therapeutic power of hypnosis with the intention to heal and reprogram these deep-rooted mental patterns.

⊛ What is Hypnohealing?

Hypnohealing is the use of **clinical hypnosis** to facilitate emotional healing and subconscious reprogramming. It taps into a deeply relaxed, suggestible state—commonly referred to as the **theta brainwave state**—where the mind becomes highly receptive to positive change.

While traditional self-help focuses on conscious habits and affirmations, Hypnohealing works **at the root**, where beliefs were first formed.

⊕ Why Working Professionals Need Hypnohealing

Let's be honest—no amount of training or certification can compensate for inner blocks like:

- "I'm not good enough to lead this project."
- "Success never lasts for me."
- "I must work harder than everyone to be respected."
- "Speaking up will make me look foolish."

These are not rational thoughts. They are **subconscious scripts**—and they play on a loop, influencing how we show up in our careers.

⬗ The Science Behind Hypnohealing

⬢ Brainwave Mechanics

In normal waking life, our brains operate in **beta waves**. But during hypnosis, brain activity slows to **theta waves**— the same state we enter just before sleep. It's here that the subconscious becomes accessible.

A study by Stanford University School of Medicine using fMRI imaging showed that hypnosis dramatically increases connectivity between the **dorsal anterior cingulate cortex** (which governs focus), the **insula** (which processes body sensations), and the **default mode network** (related to self-reflection). This allows for **deep emotional integration and belief modification**.

🧘♂️ Benefits Proven by Research:

- **50% reduction in stress** after six weeks of hypnosis sessions (Journal of Consulting and Clinical Psychology)

- **Improved cognitive flexibility and focus** (Harvard Medical School)

- **Long-term change in behavioral patterns**, such as quitting smoking or overcoming phobias

✳️ The Hypnohealing Process

Though it can feel mysterious, Hypnohealing follows a structured approach:

Step 1: Induction into Relaxed State

- Deep breathing, body scanning, and visual imagery are used to quiet the mind.

Step 2: Accessing the Subconscious

- The hypnotherapist guides the individual to a past memory or belief that holds emotional charge.

Step 3: Reprogramming

- The client is invited to release the negative association and replace it with an empowering belief.

Step 4: Visualization

- The client visualizes themselves embodying this new belief in real-life scenarios (e.g., speaking confidently, handling pressure calmly).

Step 5: Awakening and Anchoring

- The session ends with affirmations and gentle awakening, followed by journaling or reflection to reinforce the experience.

Case Study 1: Sarah – Healing Imposter Syndrome

Sarah, a high-performing Senior Manager in a global FMCG company, struggled with **imposter syndrome**. Despite multiple awards and glowing appraisals, she constantly feared being "exposed."

Her Breakthrough

During hypnotherapy, Sarah regressed to a moment in childhood when her older sibling was praised and she was told she was "not as smart." This created a belief: "I must work harder to prove I'm worthy."

Through **Hypnohealing**, she:

- Revisited the memory and offered her younger self compassion

- Replaced the belief with: *"I am inherently worthy of success"*
- Visualized herself walking into meetings with confidence and clarity

Outcome

Within two months, Sarah applied for and received a promotion.

"It felt like I had untied a knot I didn't know was choking me," she said.

🔄 Rewiring Workplace Stress Responses

Stress isn't just about deadlines—it's about **perceived danger**. The subconscious sees demanding bosses, tight timelines, or speaking in meetings as threats.

🧠 Hypnohealing Reframe

- Teaches the brain to **associate these situations with safety**
- Reduces physical stress responses by calming the nervous system

👦💼 Case Study 2: Raj – From Anxiety to Authority

Raj, a 33-year-old Financial Analyst, suffered **panic attacks before client meetings**. He had the skills, but his body betrayed him.

In hypnosis, Raj recalled a 9th-grade incident where he blanked out during a speech and was laughed at.

That embarrassment encoded a fear: "Public speaking = humiliation."

Through Hypnohealing:

- He rewrote the memory as a moment of courage instead of shame
- Adopted the belief: *"My voice matters"*
- Practiced visualization of calm, impactful presentations

Result

- His anxiety reduced by 70% in a month
- He was later asked to co-lead a high-stakes investor pitch

"I stopped dreading the stage and started owning it."

☑ Boosting Performance & Focus Through Hypnosis

The subconscious thrives on clarity and repetition. Hypnohealing enhances:

- **Goal alignment**
- **Focus and decision-making**
- **Motivation and energy management**

👦💼 Case Study 3: Neeraj – A CEO's Cognitive Upgrade

Neeraj, the founder of a mid-size tech startup, felt overwhelmed with decision fatigue. He couldn't think straight by midday and questioned his competence.

In a 3-month Hypnohealing protocol:

- He practiced 15-minute "deep state resets" daily
- Used visual scripts where he saw himself making calm, clear decisions
- Reprogrammed the belief: *"I don't have to carry everything alone"*

Result

- Reported 2x more productivity
- Delegated more effectively
- Achieved a 20% revenue increase in one quarter

🧘‍♂️💡 Self-Hypnosis: A Daily Ritual for Professionals

While working with a practitioner has benefits, professionals can also practice **self-hypnosis**. Here's how:

5-Minute Daily Hypnohealing Practice:

1. **Find Stillness**: Sit in a quiet space. Close your eyes. Breathe deeply.

2. **State the Intention**: Choose one belief to reprogram (e.g., "I can handle pressure with ease").

3. **Repeat and Visualize**: Slowly repeat the affirmation while visualizing success scenarios.

4. **Feel the Emotion**: Imagine the confidence, peace, or joy you'll feel. Let it wash over you.

5. **Return and Reflect**: Gently come back, write one insight in a journal.

Practiced consistently, this re-trains the subconscious to work **for** you instead of against you.

▦ Corporate Integration of Hypnohealing

⟨⟩ Companies Are Catching On

- **Google**: Offers daily "mind reset" sessions that include guided hypnosis techniques

- **Goldman Sachs**: Runs private stress management programs for traders using visualization

- **Salesforce**: Encourages energy clearing meditations during high-pressure quarters

💼 Corporate Use Cases

- **Leadership Retreats**: Using Hypnohealing to prepare for visioning and strategy setting

- **Change Management**: Helping teams adjust to mergers or transitions by addressing fear

- **Performance Enhancement**: Sales teams using hypnotherapy to overcome call reluctance or rejection trauma

✳ Quote

"You don't need to hustle harder. You need to heal deeper."

◎ Why It Works So Well for Professionals

Unlike surface-level mindset work, Hypnohealing deals with the **emotional residue behind behavior.**

- It helps a chronically anxious employee **release the root fear**.

- It enables a perfectionist leader to **trust delegation**.

- It supports a burnt-out founder in **creating balance without guilt**.

And most importantly, it **restores the nervous system**, allowing clarity, confidence, and calm to emerge.

💬 Final Words: Rewiring for Purposeful Success

In the relentless pace of corporate life, Hypnohealing is not a luxury—it's a **necessity for the new age professional**.

Gone are the days where grit alone could sustain growth. Today's leaders must also master their **inner landscape**.

You already have the intelligence, the education, the drive.

What you need now is **alignment**.

With Hypnohealing, you gain the ability to:

- Let go of inherited fears
- Build new mental architecture
- Step fully into your authentic power

Because when your **subconscious says yes**, the world starts saying yes too.

 Chapter 7

Tarot Life Coaching – Intuitive Guidance for Decision-Making

Introduction: Beyond Logic – The Rise of Intuitive Intelligence in the Corporate World

Every day, corporate professionals make hundreds of decisions—from navigating team dynamics to weighing business opportunities. While data and logic dominate traditional leadership paradigms, a growing number of professionals are turning inward, exploring tools that sharpen **intuition** and enhance **self-awareness**.

One such tool is **Tarot Life Coaching**—a powerful blend of symbolic insight, subconscious reflection, and intuitive guidance that helps leaders and employees alike make informed, aligned, and soulful decisions.

Far from superstition or prediction, **Tarot Life Coaching is about clarity**. It asks:

- What patterns are influencing your decisions?
- What hidden blocks are affecting your progress?
- What is your deeper truth trying to tell you?

☺ What Is Tarot Life Coaching?

Tarot Life Coaching uses tarot cards as a **mirror to the subconscious mind**. Each card is rich with imagery, archetypes, and emotional symbolism that speak directly to inner truths we may not yet have verbalized.

Unlike fortune-telling, which looks outward, **Tarot Life Coaching looks inward**. It combines traditional coaching methods (goal setting, reflection, action planning) with the **intuitive and visual language of tarot**.

✵ Key Principles of Tarot Life Coaching

1. **Intuitive Guidance**: Helping clients access their own wisdom.

2. **Symbolic Interpretation**: Using tarot cards as tools to reveal subconscious beliefs and emotional blocks.

3. **Coaching Alignment**: Combining spiritual insight with actionable, real-world decisions.

4. **Energy & Emotional Intelligence**: Addressing not just the 'what' of decisions, but the emotional energy behind them.

☏ The Science Behind Intuition and Symbolism

While tarot may seem mystical, modern psychology offers a solid foundation for why it works—especially in high-pressure environments.

 Cognitive Priming

Viewing symbolic images activates associations in the brain, priming individuals to access deeper layers of memory and emotion. When someone sees a card like the **Tower** (symbolizing upheaval), their subconscious may recall times of disruption—leading to **insightful reflection and awareness**.

Neuroplasticity and Visualization

Tarot triggers **new neural pathways** by prompting people to consider alternative perspectives, thereby enhancing emotional flexibility and problem-solving.

Heart-Brain Coherence

The HeartMath Institute has shown that intuitive intelligence—felt through the heart—often **precedes analytical thought**. Tarot taps into this by helping professionals **feel** into decisions rather than overthink them.

How Tarot Helps in the Workplace

1. Decision-Making Clarity

When professionals feel stuck between options, tarot helps clarify the **emotional and energetic implications** of each path.

2. Leadership Development

Executives use tarot to understand their strengths, shadow patterns, and leadership archetypes.

3. Career Transitions

Whether it's changing roles or industries, tarot coaching helps individuals uncover fears, hopes, and next steps.

4. Team Dynamics & Conflict Resolution

Tarot uncovers emotional undercurrents in team relationships, offering insights into empathy, ego, and communication gaps.

☕ ☿ How a Tarot Life Coaching Session Works

Step 1: Set the Intention

Begin with a powerful question such as:

- "What's blocking my growth at work?"
- "What is the next best step in my career?"
- "How can I manage conflict with my team?"

Step 2: Choose a Spread

- **1-Card Pull**: Daily guidance or a quick insight.
- **3-Card Spread**: Past–Present–Future or Situation–Challenge–Outcome.
- **Celtic Cross Spread**: A comprehensive layout ideal for major career decisions.

Step 3: Interpret the Cards

A professional Tarot Life Coach helps the client:

- Decode the symbolic imagery.
- Connect the message to real-world experiences.
- Reflect on emotional responses triggered by the reading.

Step 4: Action Plan

Translate insights into tangible next steps:

- A conversation to initiate.
- A limiting belief to release.
- A leadership approach to embody.

😊💼 Case Study 1: Priya – Should I Take That Global Role?

Background: Priya, a successful HR Director at a tech firm, was offered a leadership role in Germany. While the promotion excited her, the thought of uprooting her family triggered guilt and uncertainty.

Tarot Coaching Spread:

- **Strengths (The Magician)**: Her skills were perfectly suited.
- **Challenge (The Tower)**: Major personal life upheaval.
- **Advice (The Star)**: Trust her higher vision.
- **Outcome (The Sun)**: A joyful new chapter.

Result

Priya gained clarity. She accepted the offer, enrolled her children in international school early, and created a relocation plan with her partner. Six months in, she called it her **"soul-aligned leap."**

👦💼 Case Study 2: Rohit – Navigating Workplace Conflict

Background: Rohit, a project manager, found himself in constant friction with a senior colleague. He felt undermined and couldn't communicate effectively.

Tarot Coaching Spread:

- **Root (Five of Swords)**: Ego clashes and power struggles.

- **Solution (Temperance)**: Seek emotional balance and collaboration.

- **Outcome (Six of Pentacles)**: Reciprocity and fair give-and-take.

Result

Rohit approached the colleague not with blame, but with curiosity. They restructured their deliverables and established weekly check-ins. What was once a warzone became a partnership.

👦💼 Case Study 3: Anjali – Rediscovering Career Purpose

Background: After 15 years in brand strategy, Anjali felt stuck. She no longer felt joy in her work and feared starting over.

Tarot Coaching Spread:

- **Current Energy (The Hermit)**: Time for introspection.
- **Block (Eight of Cups)**: Fear of leaving the familiar.

- **Guidance (The Fool)**: Take a leap of faith.
- **Hidden Strength (Queen of Wands)**: Creative leadership.

Result

Anjali began freelancing on the side in a field she loved—storytelling and content creation. One year later, she launched her own brand studio.

"Tarot didn't tell me what to do. It helped me **listen to what I already knew**."

☑ Tarot in Modern Corporate Culture

Far from being taboo, tarot is quietly entering corporate well-being programs as a tool for:

- Emotional intelligence training
- Leadership coaching
- Strategic retreats
- Mindfulness & reflection sessions

Companies like **LinkedIn** and **Salesforce** have explored symbolism-based visioning sessions for creative teams. Some startups even offer tarot as part of **founder coaching** and **team bonding experiences**.

◳ Why It Works So Well for Professionals

Traditional Coaching	Tarot Life Coaching
Focuses on logic and goals	Combines logic with emotion and intuition
Works with what you know	Explores what you **feel** and don't yet know

Traditional Coaching	Tarot Life Coaching
Future-focused	Integrates **past patterns**, present energy, and future alignment
Structured questioning	Symbol-driven discovery
May ignore energetic blocks	Brings unconscious fears into the light

✳ Quote

"Tarot doesn't predict your future—it helps you create it with clarity and confidence."

The Hidden Benefits of Tarot Coaching in the Workplace

1. **Emotional Awareness**: Seeing a challenging card often unlocks emotions we weren't aware of.

2. **Creative Problem Solving**: Symbolic thinking activates the right brain and unlocks new ideas.

3. **Increased Confidence**: When a decision is made in alignment with both logic and intuition, doubt disappears.

4. **Stronger Communication**: Tarot can reveal underlying emotions in relationships, improving how we express ourselves.

How to Start Using Tarot in Your Career

- Begin with a simple daily 1-card pull:

  "What energy should I bring to work today?"

- For major decisions, try a 3-card spread:

  "What's helping me, what's hindering me, and what's the way forward?"

- Journal your thoughts. Don't just focus on the meaning—focus on **how the card makes you feel**.

- Consider working with a professional Tarot Life Coach who specializes in corporate coaching for deeper exploration.

✳ Sample Questions Professionals Can Ask in Tarot Life Coaching

- What's blocking me from stepping into leadership?

- How can I show up more confidently in meetings?

- What limiting belief is affecting my growth?

- How can I improve my team's dynamics?

- What lesson does this conflict hold for me?

- What does my career want from me next?

💬 Final Words: Trust Your Inner Compass

In a world driven by KPIs, OKRs, and data dashboards, it's easy to forget the **power of our inner compass**.

Tarot Life Coaching is not about escaping reality—it's about engaging with it more **intuitively, authentically, and powerfully**.

Whether you're a senior executive making multi-crore decisions or a young professional navigating your next move, your intuition has something to say. Tarot simply gives it a microphone.

Logic leads. Intuition reveals. When both are honored, magic happens.

Neuro-Linguistic Programming (NLP) – Rewiring the Mind for Corporate Excellence

 Introduction: The Language of Success Begins in the Mind

In today's high-pressure, results-driven corporate world, success is not just about strategy—**it's about mindset**. How we think, how we communicate, and how we perceive situations define not only our career trajectory but our experience of life itself.

Neuro-Linguistic Programming (NLP) offers a toolkit to **reprogram mental patterns**, reshape communication styles, and **align internal beliefs** with professional goals. It is the bridge between how we perceive the world and how we act within it.

Originally developed in the 1970s by Richard Bandler and John Grinder, NLP has become a popular framework for enhancing performance, leadership, and emotional intelligence in corporate environments.

"If you want to change the results, you have to change the programming."

— NLP Principle

What is NLP?

Neuro-Linguistic Programming is based on the premise that our **neurology (neuro), language (linguistic),** and **behavioral patterns (programming)** create the map we use to navigate reality. NLP helps us:

- Understand our mental "software"
- Identify and shift limiting patterns
- Enhance interpersonal effectiveness
- Model the strategies of high achievers

In short, NLP helps people understand **how they do what they do,** and offers tools to do it better.

The Science Behind NLP

Although NLP is often considered more practical than theoretical, it aligns with several cognitive science and psychology principles.

Cognitive Reframing

NLP techniques such as "reframing" are supported by cognitive behavioral therapy (CBT), which demonstrates that changing interpretation leads to behavioral change.

Neuroplasticity

Repeated use of NLP techniques can rewire neural pathways, strengthening positive habits and weakening unhelpful responses—just like affirmations or meditation.

🧑‍🤝‍🧑 Mirror Neurons and Communication

Techniques like **mirroring, rapport building**, and **anchoring** tap into how our brain empathizes and learns from others, based on the activity of mirror neurons.

❄️ Key Techniques in NLP (and How They Help Professionals)

1. Anchoring

Used to associate a specific emotional state (e.g., confidence) with a physical action (e.g., touching your wrist). Great for handling stress before meetings or public speaking.

2. Swish Pattern

A visualization technique to replace a negative pattern (e.g., fear of failure) with a positive one (e.g., vision of success).

3. Reframing

Changing the meaning you assign to an event—turning "rejection" into "redirection," for instance.

4. Rapport Building

Subtle body language and verbal mirroring to build trust and connection in conversations—crucial in team leadership and sales.

5. Meta Model & Milton Model

Powerful questioning frameworks to either clarify vague thoughts (Meta) or induce relaxation and suggestion (Milton).

😊💼 Case Study 1: Ananya – From Stage Fright to Stage Star

Background

Ananya, a 34-year-old Business Development Manager at a tech company, was brilliant in one-on-one conversations but froze during presentations.

NLP Intervention

- Used **anchoring** to link confidence with a subtle breath gesture

- Practiced the **swish pattern** by mentally replacing the image of a judgmental audience with one of smiling, supportive faces

Result

Ananya transformed her fear into excitement. Within a month, she was confidently presenting at a leadership summit, earning praise from her team and management.

"It wasn't just practice—it was how I reprogrammed my emotional response that changed everything."

😊💼 Case Study 2: Vikram – Rewriting the Rejection Narrative

Background

Vikram, a mid-level manager in a finance firm, applied for an internal promotion and was rejected. He took it personally and began withdrawing from projects.

NLP Coaching Focus

Reframing: Vikram learned to see the rejection not as failure but as feedback

Uncovered a childhood memory of never being "chosen" and applied **timeline therapy** to reprocess that experience

Result

He began volunteering for cross-functional roles again and eventually landed a more senior role in another department that better suited his skills.

💬 NLP in Leadership and Team Management

Leaders trained in NLP can:

- Build **instant rapport** with diverse teams
- **Resolve conflicts** by understanding underlying mental maps
- Use **precision language** to inspire and influence
- Increase **team motivation** through values alignment

👦💼 Case Study 3: Meera – Transforming Toxic Culture

Background

Meera, a Senior VP in a retail chain, faced employee disengagement and communication gaps in her team.

NLP Approach

- Conducted **values elicitation** sessions to understand team motivations

- Used **mirroring** in conversations to build trust

- Trained team leads in **language precision** to avoid miscommunication

Result

Within 4 months, the team's engagement score rose by 38%, and turnover dropped by half.

⊛ NLP for Career Growth and Personal Mastery

Many professionals hit an invisible ceiling—not due to lack of talent, but due to subconscious programming like:

- "I'm not good enough."
- "I'm too old to start over."
- "I'm not a people person."

NLP helps by:

- Identifying root beliefs
- Visualizing new patterns of success
- Creating mental strategies used by top performers

▨ Sample NLP Exercise: "Rewriting a Limiting Belief"

Step 1: Identify the Belief

Example: "I always choke under pressure."

Step 2: Notice the Origin

When did this start? What was the first experience?

Step 3: Swish Pattern

- Imagine the negative outcome (choking in a meeting) as a mental image

- Shrink it, fade it, move it away

- Replace it with a compelling visual of you speaking with ease

- Repeat 10 times with speed and emotion

Step 4: Anchor the New State

While visualizing success, press your thumb and middle finger together to "lock in" the emotion.

NLP in Corporate Wellness and Coaching

Forward-thinking companies are integrating NLP into:

- **Executive coaching** programs
- **Sales training** for persuasion and objection handling
- **Conflict resolution** frameworks
- **Employee wellness** initiatives to manage stress and anxiety

Organizations Using NLP Techniques:

- **Intel** and **IBM** include NLP in leadership development
- **Tony Robbins**, whose training programs are NLP-based, regularly coaches CEOs and celebrities
- HR consultancies worldwide use NLP in behavior-based interview frameworks

✨ Why NLP Resonates with Today's Professionals

- **Fast Results**: Change doesn't require months of therapy

- **Customizable**: Works across industries, roles, and seniority levels

- **Empowering**: Gives professionals tools to self-regulate, not depend on external motivation

✳ Quote

*"If you change the way you speak to yourself,
you change your world."*

◎ Real Benefits Experienced by Corporate Professionals

Challenge	NLP Transformation
Fear of public speaking	Anchoring confidence through body cues
Negative self-talk	Belief reprogramming via affirmations
Lack of motivation	Eliciting core values to ignite purpose
Difficult clients	Reframing resistance into unmet needs
Communication gaps	Using rapport and matching language

💬 Final Words: A Mind Aligned is a Life Transformed

Neuro-Linguistic Programming isn't about tricks or manipulation—it's about **awareness**. Awareness of how your thoughts shape your actions. Awareness of how your language defines your reality. Awareness of how your internal map can either keep you trapped or guide you to freedom.

With NLP, professionals are no longer victims of old programming. They become **architects of new possibility**.

Whether you're a leader looking to inspire, a professional looking to grow, or an individual looking to feel more in control, NLP equips you with the tools to think better, speak better, and live better.

Because your future isn't written—it's programmed.

And you hold the keyboard.

Chapter 9

Integrating these Modalities into Daily Corporate Life

Creating a Culture of Conscious Leadership and Lasting Well-Being

🚀 A Corporate World at a Crossroads

There was a time when the corporate world measured success purely by numbers: quarterly profits, stock valuations, performance metrics. But today, we're facing a new reality. Mental health issues are soaring. Burnout is no longer an exception—it's an epidemic. The "great resignation" and quiet quitting trends have sent shockwaves across industries.

Employees are no longer content with paychecks alone—they're seeking purpose, balance, and emotional well-being. Leaders are being challenged to move beyond managing productivity to nurturing **human potential**.

And that's where spiritual modalities step in—not as mystical alternatives, but as **powerful, science-backed tools** that unlock emotional intelligence, reduce stress, enhance creativity, and foster authentic leadership.

🧠 The Science of Holistic Workplace Wellness

Studies from institutions like the **American Psychological Association (APA)**, **Harvard Business Review**, and **Stanford School of Medicine** have repeatedly shown:

- **Emotionally intelligent leaders** build more productive and loyal teams.
- **Mindfulness and energy practices** reduce stress hormone levels and increase brain plasticity.
- **Workplaces that prioritize emotional health** see 3X higher employee engagement and retention.

Companies like Google, Intel, and Salesforce are no longer treating well-being as a perk—it's becoming a strategic priority.

🧠 Let's Explore How Each Modality Can Be Seamlessly Integrated

☐ Emotional Freedom Technique (EFT) – Your Daily Stress Reset

EFT, or tapping, is an efficient, quick, and **cost-effective** stress-reduction technique. Think of it as a psychological circuit breaker that clears emotional overwhelm.

📌 How to Integrate EFT

- **Tapping Corners in Breakout Zones**: Calm pods or EFT spaces in office wellness areas.
- **Pre-Pitch Rituals**: A 3-minute tapping round before high-stakes meetings or client calls.
- **Weekly "Release & Recharge" Workshops**: Conducted by certified EFT coaches to reduce cumulative stress.

👦💻 Case Study

At Luminate Tech, developers tapped before major code deployment. Within three months, reported stress dropped by 35% and cross-functional collaboration improved drastically.

"It gave our logical minds a way to soothe our emotional systems."

– CTO, Luminate Tech

2️⃣ Past Life Regression (PLR) – Unlocking Subconscious Career Blocks

PLR may sound unconventional, but it works at the level of the **subconscious mind** where most fears and patterns are rooted. Whether or not one believes in literal past lives, the metaphors and memories revealed often provide profound psychological insight.

📌 How to Integrate PLR

- **PLR-Inspired Visualization**: Deep meditations that help professionals reconnect with inner wisdom.

- **One-on-One Corporate Coaching**: Used with senior leaders who face chronic self-doubt or fear of failure.

- **Insight Retreats**: Guided PLR sessions during offsites to encourage deep emotional processing.

👦💼 Case Study

Tanya, a high-potential VP, repeatedly froze during board presentations. A PLR-inspired regression revealed a memory where being outspoken had caused public humiliation. Once processed, she became one of the firm's most persuasive voices.

"I didn't just heal a fear—I reclaimed my voice."

3️⃣ Shadow Work – Transforming Leaders from the Inside Out

Shadow Work helps uncover the **blind spots** we all carry—emotions we repress, traits we disown, behaviors we justify. In corporate terms, this translates to improved emotional intelligence, reduced conflict, and stronger team dynamics.

📌 How to Integrate Shadow Work:

- **360° Feedback + Shadow Integration**: Encourage leaders to reflect on recurring interpersonal feedback.

- **Conflict Coaching**: Use shadow principles to resolve tension by helping parties own their projections.

- **Leadership Circles**: Peer support spaces for identifying and integrating hidden fears and emotional wounds.

👦💼 Case Study

Arjun, a micromanaging COO, was blind to how his need for control stemmed from early trauma. Shadow coaching revealed this inner script. He learned to trust his team—and revenue grew 20% under his more empowering leadership.

"The part of me I was ashamed of turned out to be my greatest teacher."

4️⃣ Hypnohealing – Reprogramming the Mental Operating System

In high-stakes roles, professionals often operate with outdated internal software—fear of speaking, pressure to prove themselves, fear of rejection. Hypnohealing accesses the **theta brainwave state,** ideal for deep rewiring.

📌 How to Integrate Hypnohealing:

- **Self-Hypnosis Modules**: 10-minute audio tracks employees can use before performance reviews, sales pitches, or creative brainstorming.

- **Executive Coaching Add-On**: Combine traditional coaching with subconscious reprogramming for greater results.

- **Sleep Wellness Programs**: Use hypnohealing to improve rest and reduce burnout.

👦💼 Case Study

Neha, a product strategist at a Fortune 500 firm, used hypnohealing to overcome procrastination. Within six weeks, her output doubled, and she led the launch of one of the company's most successful products.

5️⃣ Tarot Life Coaching – Intuition Meets Intelligence

Tarot is not about predicting the future; it's about understanding your present with **depth and objectivity.** The symbolic language of tarot taps into the subconscious, helping professionals gain clarity during transitions, conflict, or decision paralysis.

📌 How to Integrate Tarot Life Coaching

- **Quarterly Leadership Check-Ins**: Using tarot as part of reflective coaching conversations.

- **Innovation Labs**: Pull a tarot card to stimulate unconventional perspectives before brainstorming.

- **Visioning Retreats**: Cards used for strategic foresight and intuitive alignment.

🧑💼 Case Study

Ritesh, a creative director, was at a career crossroads. Through tarot coaching, he discovered he was operating from fear rather than vision. The guidance helped him pivot into a new vertical—and revenue from the division soared 45% in a year.

"Tarot didn't give me answers. It gave me better questions."

5. NLP – Language that Rewires Leadership

NLP, or Neuro-Linguistic Programming, is the art of understanding how language, thought patterns, and behavior shape outcomes. In the corporate world, NLP becomes a performance amplifier, empowering professionals to shift limiting beliefs, communicate with precision, and lead with influence.

Rather than focusing on "what" people do, NLP reveals the "how"—how they think, how they process information, and how they can reprogram themselves for success. It's about consciously designing mental strategies that lead to better choices, clearer communication, and higher achievement.

📌 How to Integrate NLP into Corporate Life:

- Leadership Influence Workshops: Train managers and team leads in language patterns, rapport building, and anchoring techniques to boost team morale and performance.

- Sales & Client Negotiation Labs: Use NLP to decode client communication styles and match them to increase trust and conversions.

- Behavioral Coaching for Performance Blocks: Help employees reframe fears, overcome imposter syndrome, and model excellence from top performers using NLP modeling.

🧑💼 Case Study

Neelam, a senior operations head at a logistics firm, was struggling with high attrition and low morale within her team. Despite her efforts, her communication often came across as controlling and abrupt. An NLP-based coaching intervention helped her uncover her core pattern of communicating from a place of anxiety and control.

Through NLP techniques like reframing, anchoring, and meta-model questioning, she began to shift her tone, adjust her message to suit different team personalities, and develop a more empowering language.

The results were profound:

- Engagement scores rose by 30%

- Conflict instances dropped significantly

- Her department exceeded their quarterly targets for the first time in two years

"NLP didn't just change how I spoke to my team—it changed how I saw them and myself."

♟♀ How to Build a Culture That Embraces These Modalities

1. **Normalize Inner Work**: Offer optional sessions, framing them as "mental fitness" rather than therapy.

2. **Train Internal Champions**: Encourage HR and leadership to undergo certification in 1–2 modalities.

3. **Make It Safe & Sacred**: Create environments where vulnerability isn't punished, but honored.

4. **Integrate Gradually**: Start with mindfulness, then expand to EFT or shadow work.

5. **Measure Outcomes**: Track stress levels, engagement scores, retention, and productivity post-programs.

✣ Corporate Benefits At a Glance

Modality	Primary Benefit	Ideal For
EFT	Stress release, emotional grounding	All employees
PLR	Removing deep-rooted blocks	Executives, creative roles
Shadow Work	Emotional intelligence, leadership growth	Mid-senior management

Modality	Primary Benefit	Ideal For
Hypnohealing	Mental clarity, focus, habit change	High-pressure roles
Tarot Coaching	Strategic insight, confidence, clarity	Founders, managers in transition
NLP	Behavioral change, communication mastery	Sales teams, leaders, performance-driven professionals

🌐 Future-Ready Workplaces Are Conscious Workplaces

Gone are the days when work and well-being were seen as separate spheres. The **corporate leaders of tomorrow** are healers, visionaries, and consciousness architects. By integrating these healing modalities, organizations are not just creating happier workplaces—they're cultivating **resilient ecosystems** where innovation, authenticity, and human potential thrive.

✅ Conclusion: The New Language of Corporate Wellness

This chapter is not an invitation to abandon logic—it's an invitation to **expand beyond it**. To embrace a language that speaks to both the head and the heart. To build cultures that nourish not just performance but **purpose**.

And as you've seen through every case study—when you do, miracles happen: careers shift, teams harmonize, leadership transforms, and businesses grow with soul.

Chapter 10

A Working Professional's Transformation Plan - A Step-by-Step Blueprint for Inner Alignment and Outer Success

Introduction: The Need for a Personal Operating System

Every high-performing company has a well-defined operating system. But what about individuals? Most working professionals run on default patterns: old conditioning, unmanaged stress, unclear goals, and internal sabotage. If left unchecked, this leads to burnout, stagnation, and disconnection from purpose.

This chapter is your **personal upgrade manual**—a structured, science-backed, soul-aligned blueprint that integrates all the modalities discussed: **EFT, PLR, Shadow Work, Hypnohealing, Tarot Life Coaching, and NLP.**

Designed to work over **90 days**, it's flexible enough to be integrated into busy corporate routines and powerful enough to **transform your emotional health, performance, leadership, and career trajectory.**

Now, you may choose to follow some of the processes or all of the processes suggested and outlined below, It's alright!

Choose a pattern that you are comfortable with and allow your mind to expand and fit the schedule into it. Once you start noticing the shift in your energy levels and performance, you will get hooked!

The 90-Day Transformation Plan: Phases of Inner Work

Phase	Duration	Focus	Core Modalities
1. Awakening	Days 1–30	Awareness & Grounding	EFT, Shadow Work, Tarot
2. Deep Seeking	Days 31–60	Subconscious Healing	PLR, Hypnohealing, Shadow
3. Alignment	Days 61–90	Peak Performance & Clarity	NLP, Tarot, EFT

Each week includes:

- 3 Micro Practices (5–15 mins)
- 1 Weekly Deep Dive (30–45 mins)
- 1 Reflection Day

Daily Practices for Transformation

Morning Ritual (15 mins)

- **Gratitude Journaling** (3 things you're grateful for)

- **EFT Round** (Target one emotion—stress, self-doubt, etc.)
- **NLP Affirmation Looping**

"I am calm, focused, and in control of my energy."

☼ Midday Reset (10 mins)

- **Mindful Break** – 5-min silent reflection or guided hypnosis
- **Tarot 1-Card Pull** – Question: "What's my focus energy now?"
- **Shadow Check-In** – "What am I avoiding/denying today?"

☽ Evening Reflection (20 mins)

- **Journaling** – Wins, triggers, emotional shifts
- **Self-Hypnosis** or **Guided Hypnohealing** Audio
- **Reframe & Visualize Tomorrow** (NLP-style future pacing)

🗃 Weekly Structure

Day	Focus	Modality
Mon	Set Intentions & Emotional Goals	EFT, Tarot
Tue	Reprogram Limiting Beliefs	NLP, Hypnohealing
Wed	Shadow Dive (Journaling or Voice Note)	Shadow Work
Thu	Visualization & Creative Flow	Tarot, PLR

Day	Focus	Modality
Fri	Weekly Review & Self-Acknowledgment	Hypnohealing
Sat	1-Hr Deep Dive (Past Life Regression or Deep Hypnosis)	PLR, Hypnohealing
Sun	Rest + Play + Reflect	Light tapping + Tarot + Grounding

🔍 Phase 1: Awakening (Days 1–30)

Objective

Build awareness, emotional grounding, and energetic balance.

Key Practices

- Daily EFT tapping for common triggers: deadlines, self-judgment, imposter syndrome.

- Start a Shadow Journal: Track emotional reactions at work.

- Begin Tarot micro-check-ins to strengthen intuition.

- Learn basic NLP techniques: Anchoring confidence before presentations.

Mini-Milestone: Increased emotional regulation, better sleep, improved focus, more self-awareness in team interactions.

🔍 Phase 2: Deep Seeking (Days 31–60)

Objective

Uncover and heal subconscious patterns and emotional wounds.

Key Practices

- One weekly PLR session (guided or audio-based) to uncover origin of fears (e.g., fear of speaking, authority conflict).

- Hypnohealing every alternate evening (track themes: confidence, self-worth, clarity).

- Deeper shadow explorations—link present triggers to past experiences (both this and prior lifetimes).

- NLP Reframing: Turn "I must prove myself" into "I choose to express my value."

Mini-Milestone: Greater emotional insight, improved relationships, deeper connection to purpose, reduction in recurring patterns.

🔍 Phase 3: Alignment (Days 61–90)

Objective

Refine, realign, and rewire your belief systems for peak clarity and consistent action.

Key Practices

- NLP-based Vision Mapping: Define your career + personal blueprint.

- Tarot-based decision-making support: Major shifts? Pull insights before big moves.

- Use EFT proactively: Tap for focus, courage, delegation, or visibility.

- Hypnohealing "future self" protocol: Integrate new identity of self-assured, peaceful, high-performing professional.

Mini-Milestone: Clarity in long-term direction, better boundaries, increased visibility, renewed excitement in career and life.

✦ Real-Life Blueprint Application: Case Vignettes

Case 1: Shalini – Burnt Out Tech Lead Turned Soulful Innovator

Before: Shalini, 38, led a backend tech team, stuck in endless code loops and stress spirals.

After: Through EFT and PLR, she released anxiety and reconnected with her deeper creative spark. With tarot + NLP work, she restructured her workflow, pitched an AI-powered product, and became a sought-after innovation coach internally.

Case 2: Dev – Sales Director Who Found His Voice

Before: Dev, a mid-level sales manager, carried anxiety around public speaking and assertiveness.

After: With Shadow Work, he discovered a deep fear of rejection from childhood. Hypnohealing and NLP gave him the tools to anchor confidence and rewire his self-talk. Today, he leads national sales calls with poise.

🏁 90-Day Milestone Review Checklist

- ☑ Emotional mastery in high-pressure scenarios
- ☑ Confidence in decision-making
- ☑ Improved communication and leadership presence
- ☑ Enhanced creativity and innovation
- ☑ Aligned sense of purpose and long-term clarity
- ☑ Reduced absenteeism, better health, improved work-life balance

🍃 Conclusion: Your Success Is an Inside-Out Process

This transformation blueprint isn't a motivational plan—it's a **practical integration of ancient wisdom and modern science.** It's not just about getting more done—it's about becoming more aligned, more peaceful, and more powerful in who you are.

The workplace of the future demands self-aware leaders, emotionally balanced teams, and purpose-driven performance.

This plan is your toolkit. The modalities are your compass. And the next 90 days? They can be the most liberating, productive, and transformational days of your professional life.

 Chapter 11

The Shift Towards a Spiritually Conscious Workplace

Transforming Corporate Culture Through Emotional, Energetic, and Spiritual Intelligence

In the ever-evolving corporate ecosystem, success is no longer defined solely by bottom lines or KPIs. Modern organizations are waking up to a new paradigm—where productivity is not divorced from personal well-being, and where performance is intricately tied to purpose. The rise of burnout, disengagement, and silent attrition has triggered a much-needed introspection: What if the way to sustainable performance is through inner alignment? Enter the spiritually conscious workplace.

The Case for Organizational Spiritual Intelligence

A spiritually conscious workplace doesn't imply religiosity. Rather, it is about fostering emotional intelligence, self-awareness, compassion, authenticity, and a connection to higher purpose. According to a report by Deloitte, companies that focus on holistic employee well-being witness 37% lower absenteeism, 21% higher productivity, and a 3.5 times greater likelihood of retaining top talent. Spiritual intelligence nurtures creativity, collaboration, and conscious leadership—qualities essential for thriving in the new world of work.

Why the Current System is Failing

Despite wellness programs, yoga days, and resilience talks, employees remain overstimulated and underconnected. The missing ingredient? Depth. Most interventions scratch the surface—offering quick fixes instead of sustainable transformation. Without addressing the subconscious fears, unresolved traumas, and suppressed emotions of the workforce, true change remains elusive.

The New Pillars of Training & Development

To usher in this shift, organizations must elevate their learning and development (L&D) strategy to include emotional and spiritual healing modalities. Below are the key areas where such modalities can be incorporated:

- Emotional Freedom Technique (EFT): For stress relief, emotional reset, and increasing focus before presentations or critical tasks.

- Past Life Regression (PLR): To release deep-seated fears or patterns that limit leadership effectiveness or risk-taking.

- Shadow Work: To improve conflict resolution, leadership self-awareness, and emotional intelligence.

- Hypnohealing: For habit transformation, mental clarity, overcoming imposter syndrome, and sleep improvement.
- Tarot Life Coaching: To strengthen intuitive decision-making and strategic clarity in ambiguity.
- Neuro-Linguistic Programming (NLP): To refine communication, overcome limiting beliefs, and model peak performers.

Implementation Strategies for a Spiritually Aligned Culture

1. Leadership Buy-In: Start with immersive workshops for top executives. Leaders must experience these modalities to champion them authentically.

2. Holistic Wellness Modules: Integrate these practices into onboarding, mid-career growth journeys, and leadership pipelines.

3. Dedicated Healing Spaces: Create mindfulness and tapping rooms for employees to recharge.

4. Certified Internal Coaches: Train HR professionals or wellness ambassadors in modalities like EFT or NLP.

5. Monthly Energy Audits: Use anonymous surveys and tarot group circles to gauge collective emotional health.

6. Partner with Transformation Experts: Collaborate with certified coaches, hypnotherapists, and shadow facilitators to build structured programs.

Case Studies of Corporate Integration

At a mid-sized IT services firm in Pune, EFT and Hypnohealing were introduced as part of the stress management curriculum. The result? A 28% reduction in stress-related leaves and a 15% increase in employee satisfaction within 90 days.

A global apparel brand offered PLR sessions to senior management as part of their quarterly offsites. One executive uncovered a past-life experience that unblocked her fear of public speaking—eventually leading her to become a regional spokesperson.

A fintech startup used Tarot Life Coaching during team visioning exercises. The symbolic insights led to faster consensus and a 40% increase in creative idea generation during product sprints.

Conclusion: Consciousness is the Future of Corporate Growth

Spiritual intelligence is no longer optional—it's strategic. Companies that recognize the human behind the role, the soul behind the skillset, and the emotion behind the effort will lead the future. By making healing a leadership skill, and integrating modalities like EFT, PLR, NLP, and more into their DNA, organizations won't just grow—they'll evolve.

The spiritual corporate is not a myth—it's a movement. And this chapter is your invitation to lead it.

Chapter 12

DIY EFT Tapping Scripts for Working Professionals for Phenomenal Career Growth

1. TAPPING FOR DAILY WORKPLACE STRESS

1. Karate Chop Point (Setup)

Even though I'm dealing with [issue], I deeply and completely love and accept myself.

Even though it feels overwhelming, I honor how I feel and am open to change.

Even though this [issue] is affecting my peace, I allow myself to let go and trust the process.

2. Negative Round (Acknowledge the Issue)

Eyebrow: This [issue] is really getting to me.

Side of Eye: I feel so caught up in it.

Under Eye: It's draining my energy and focus.

Under Nose: I don't know how to handle it.

Chin: It's always there in the back of my mind.

Collarbone: I'm tired of this stress.

Under Arm: I just want relief.

Top of Head: This pressure feels so heavy.

3.   Neutral Round (Shifting the Energy)

Eyebrow: Maybe it's okay to feel this way.

Side of Eye: I'm learning to manage it better.

Under Eye: I don't have to fix everything right now.

Under Nose: I'm allowed to take small steps.

Chin: What if this could get easier?

Collarbone: I'm open to finding peace.

Under Arm: I give myself space to breathe.

Top of Head: I am supporting myself in this moment.

4.   Positive Round (Reframe and Empower)

Eyebrow: I choose to feel calm and confident.

Side of Eye: I am capable of handling this.

Under Eye: I trust my process.

Under Nose: I honor my growth.

Chin: I am stronger than this challenge.

Collarbone: I am finding clarity and peace.

Under Arm: I am stepping into my power.

Top of Head: I deeply and completely love and accept myself.

2.   TAPPING FOR OVERWHELM AND TOO MANY RESPONSIBILITIES

1.   Karate Chop Point (Setup)

Even though I'm dealing with [issue], I deeply and completely love and accept myself.

Even though it feels overwhelming, I honor how I feel and am open to change.

Even though this [issue] is affecting my peace, I allow myself to let go and trust the process.

2.   Negative Round (Acknowledge the Issue)

Eyebrow: This [issue] is really getting to me.

Side of Eye: I feel so caught up in it.

Under Eye: It's draining my energy and focus.

Under Nose: I don't know how to handle it.

Chin: It's always there in the back of my mind.

Collarbone: I'm tired of this stress.

Under Arm: I just want relief.

Top of Head: This pressure feels so heavy.

3.   Neutral Round (Shifting the Energy)

Eyebrow: Maybe it's okay to feel this way.

Side of Eye: I'm learning to manage it better.

Under Eye: I don't have to fix everything right now.

Under Nose: I'm allowed to take small steps.

Chin: What if this could get easier?

Collarbone: I'm open to finding peace.

Under Arm: I give myself space to breathe.

Top of Head: I am supporting myself in this moment.

4. Positive Round (Reframe and Empower)

Eyebrow: I choose to feel calm and confident.

Side of Eye: I am capable of handling this.

Under Eye: I trust my process.

Under Nose: I honor my growth.

Chin: I am stronger than this challenge.

Collarbone: I am finding clarity and peace.

Under Arm: I am stepping into my power.

Top of Head: I deeply and completely love and accept myself.

3. Tapping for Monday Morning Anxiety

1. Karate Chop Point (Setup)

Even though I'm dealing with [issue], I deeply and completely love and accept myself.

Even though it feels overwhelming, I honor how I feel and am open to change.

Even though this [issue] is affecting my peace, I allow myself to let go and trust the process.

2. Negative Round (Acknowledge the Issue)

Eyebrow: This [issue] is really getting to me.

Side of Eye: I feel so caught up in it.

Under Eye: It's draining my energy and focus.

Under Nose: I don't know how to handle it.

Chin: It's always there in the back of my mind.

Collarbone: I'm tired of this stress.

Under Arm: I just want relief.

Top of Head: This pressure feels so heavy.

3. Neutral Round (Shifting the Energy)

Eyebrow: Maybe it's okay to feel this way.

Side of Eye: I'm learning to manage it better.

Under Eye: I don't have to fix everything right now.

Under Nose: I'm allowed to take small steps.

Chin: What if this could get easier?

Collarbone: I'm open to finding peace.

Under Arm: I give myself space to breathe.

Top of Head: I am supporting myself in this moment.

4.   Positive Round (Reframe and Empower)

Eyebrow: I choose to feel calm and confident.

Side of Eye: I am capable of handling this.

Under Eye: I trust my process.

Under Nose: I honor my growth.

Chin: I am stronger than this challenge.

Collarbone: I am finding clarity and peace.

Under Arm: I am stepping into my power.

Top of Head: I deeply and completely love and accept myself.

4. TAPPING FOR END-OF-DAY MENTAL FATIGUE

1.   Karate Chop Point (Setup)

Even though I'm dealing with [issue], I deeply and completely love and accept myself.

Even though it feels overwhelming, I honor how I feel and am open to change.

Even though this [issue] is affecting my peace, I allow myself to let go and trust the process.

2.   Negative Round (Acknowledge the Issue)

Eyebrow: This [issue] is really getting to me.

Side of Eye: I feel so caught up in it.

Under Eye: It's draining my energy and focus.

Under Nose: I don't know how to handle it.

Chin: It's always there in the back of my mind.

Collarbone: I'm tired of this stress.

Under Arm: I just want relief.

Top of Head: This pressure feels so heavy.

3.   Neutral Round (Shifting the Energy)

Eyebrow: Maybe it's okay to feel this way.

Side of Eye: I'm learning to manage it better.

Under Eye: I don't have to fix everything right now.

Under Nose: I'm allowed to take small steps.

Chin: What if this could get easier?

Collarbone: I'm open to finding peace.

Under Arm: I give myself space to breathe.

Top of Head: I am supporting myself in this moment.

4.   Positive Round (Reframe and Empower)

Eyebrow: I choose to feel calm and confident.

Side of Eye: I am capable of handling this.

Under Eye: I trust my process.

Under Nose: I honor my growth.

Chin: I am stronger than this challenge.

Collarbone: I am finding clarity and peace.

Under Arm: I am stepping into my power.

Top of Head: I deeply and completely love and accept myself.

5. TAPPING FOR FEAR OF JOB LOSS

1. Karate Chop Point (Setup)

Even though I'm dealing with [issue], I deeply and completely love and accept myself.

Even though it feels overwhelming, I honor how I feel and am open to change.

Even though this [issue] is affecting my peace, I allow myself to let go and trust the process.

2. Negative Round (Acknowledge the Issue)

Eyebrow: This [issue] is really getting to me.

Side of Eye: I feel so caught up in it.

Under Eye: It's draining my energy and focus.

Under Nose: I don't know how to handle it.

Chin: It's always there in the back of my mind.

Collarbone: I'm tired of this stress.

Under Arm: I just want relief.

Top of Head: This pressure feels so heavy.

3. Neutral Round (Shifting the Energy)

Eyebrow: Maybe it's okay to feel this way.

Side of Eye: I'm learning to manage it better.

Under Eye: I don't have to fix everything right now.

Under Nose: I'm allowed to take small steps.

Chin: What if this could get easier?

Collarbone: I'm open to finding peace.

Under Arm: I give myself space to breathe.

Top of Head: I am supporting myself in this moment.

4.   Positive Round (Reframe and Empower)

Eyebrow: I choose to feel calm and confident.

Side of Eye: I am capable of handling this.

Under Eye: I trust my process.

Under Nose: I honor my growth.

Chin: I am stronger than this challenge.

Collarbone: I am finding clarity and peace.

Under Arm: I am stepping into my power.

Top of Head: I deeply and completely love and accept myself.

6.   TAPPING FOR FEELING STUCK IN CAREER

1.   Karate Chop Point (Setup)

Even though I'm dealing with [issue], I deeply and completely love and accept myself.

Even though it feels overwhelming, I honor how I feel and am open to change.

Even though this [issue] is affecting my peace, I allow myself to let go and trust the process.

2.   Negative Round (Acknowledge the Issue)

Eyebrow: This [issue] is really getting to me.

Side of Eye: I feel so caught up in it.

Under Eye: It's draining my energy and focus.

Under Nose: I don't know how to handle it.

Chin: It's always there in the back of my mind.

Collarbone: I'm tired of this stress.

Under Arm: I just want relief.

Top of Head: This pressure feels so heavy.

3.   Neutral Round (Shifting the Energy)

Eyebrow: Maybe it's okay to feel this way.

Side of Eye: I'm learning to manage it better.

Under Eye: I don't have to fix everything right now.

Under Nose: I'm allowed to take small steps.

Chin: What if this could get easier?

Collarbone: I'm open to finding peace.

Under Arm: I give myself space to breathe.

Top of Head: I am supporting myself in this moment.

4.   Positive Round (Reframe and Empower)

Eyebrow: I choose to feel calm and confident.

Side of Eye: I am capable of handling this.

Under Eye: I trust my process.

Under Nose: I honor my growth.

Chin: I am stronger than this challenge.

Collarbone: I am finding clarity and peace.

Under Arm: I am stepping into my power.

Top of Head: I deeply and completely love and accept myself.

7.   TAPPING FOR LACK OF MOTIVATION

1.   Karate Chop Point (Setup)

Even though I'm dealing with [issue], I deeply and completely love and accept myself.

Even though it feels overwhelming, I honor how I feel and am open to change.

Even though this [issue] is affecting my peace, I allow myself to let go and trust the process.

2.   Negative Round (Acknowledge the Issue)

Eyebrow: This [issue] is really getting to me.

Side of Eye: I feel so caught up in it.

Under Eye: It's draining my energy and focus.

Under Nose: I don't know how to handle it.

Chin: It's always there in the back of my mind.

Collarbone: I'm tired of this stress.

Under Arm: I just want relief.

Top of Head: This pressure feels so heavy.

3.   Neutral Round (Shifting the Energy)

Eyebrow: Maybe it's okay to feel this way.

Side of Eye: I'm learning to manage it better.

Under Eye: I don't have to fix everything right now.

Under Nose: I'm allowed to take small steps.

Chin: What if this could get easier?

Collarbone: I'm open to finding peace.

Under Arm: I give myself space to breathe.

Top of Head: I am supporting myself in this moment.

4.   Positive Round (Reframe and Empower)

Eyebrow: I choose to feel calm and confident.

Side of Eye: I am capable of handling this.

Under Eye: I trust my process.

Under Nose: I honor my growth.

Chin: I am stronger than this challenge.

Collarbone: I am finding clarity and peace.

Under Arm: I am stepping into my power.

Top of Head: I deeply and completely love and accept myself.

8.   TAPPING FOR FEAR OF FAILURE OR TAKING RISKS

1.   Karate Chop Point (Setup)

Even though I'm dealing with [issue], I deeply and completely love and accept myself.

Even though it feels overwhelming, I honor how I feel and am open to change.

Even though this [issue] is affecting my peace, I allow myself to let go and trust the process.

2.   Negative Round (Acknowledge the Issue)

Eyebrow: This [issue] is really getting to me.

Side of Eye: I feel so caught up in it.

Under Eye: It's draining my energy and focus.

Under Nose: I don't know how to handle it.

Chin: It's always there in the back of my mind.

Collarbone: I'm tired of this stress.

Under Arm: I just want relief.

Top of Head: This pressure feels so heavy.

3. Neutral Round (Shifting the Energy)

Eyebrow: Maybe it's okay to feel this way.

Side of Eye: I'm learning to manage it better.

Under Eye: I don't have to fix everything right now.

Under Nose: I'm allowed to take small steps.

Chin: What if this could get easier?

Collarbone: I'm open to finding peace.

Under Arm: I give myself space to breathe.

Top of Head: I am supporting myself in this moment.

4. Positive Round (Reframe and Empower)

Eyebrow: I choose to feel calm and confident.

Side of Eye: I am capable of handling this.

Under Eye: I trust my process.

Under Nose: I honor my growth.

Chin: I am stronger than this challenge.

Collarbone: I am finding clarity and peace.

Under Arm: I am stepping into my power.

Top of Head: I deeply and completely love and accept myself.

9.   TAPPING FOR IMPOSTOR SYNDROME

1.   Karate Chop Point (Setup)

Even though I'm dealing with [issue], I deeply and completely love and accept myself.

Even though it feels overwhelming, I honor how I feel and am open to change.

Even though this [issue] is affecting my peace, I allow myself to let go and trust the process.

2.   Negative Round (Acknowledge the Issue)

Eyebrow: This [issue] is really getting to me.

Side of Eye: I feel so caught up in it.

Under Eye: It's draining my energy and focus.

Under Nose: I don't know how to handle it.

Chin: It's always there in the back of my mind.

Collarbone: I'm tired of this stress.

Under Arm: I just want relief.

Top of Head: This pressure feels so heavy.

3.   Neutral Round (Shifting the Energy)

Eyebrow: Maybe it's okay to feel this way.

Side of Eye: I'm learning to manage it better.

Under Eye: I don't have to fix everything right now.

Under Nose: I'm allowed to take small steps.

Chin: What if this could get easier?

Collarbone: I'm open to finding peace.

Under Arm: I give myself space to breathe.

Top of Head: I am supporting myself in this moment.

4.   Positive Round (Reframe and Empower)

Eyebrow: I choose to feel calm and confident.

Side of Eye: I am capable of handling this.

Under Eye: I trust my process.

Under Nose: I honor my growth.

Chin: I am stronger than this challenge.

Collarbone: I am finding clarity and peace.

Under Arm: I am stepping into my power.

Top of Head: I deeply and completely love and accept myself.

10. TAPPING FOR DECISION-MAKING CLARITY

1. Karate Chop Point (Setup)

Even though I'm dealing with [issue], I deeply and completely love and accept myself.

Even though it feels overwhelming, I honor how I feel and am open to change.

Even though this [issue] is affecting my peace, I allow myself to let go and trust the process.

2. Negative Round (Acknowledge the Issue)

Eyebrow: This [issue] is really getting to me.

Side of Eye: I feel so caught up in it.

Under Eye: It's draining my energy and focus.

Under Nose: I don't know how to handle it.

Chin: It's always there in the back of my mind.

Collarbone: I'm tired of this stress.

Under Arm: I just want relief.

Top of Head: This pressure feels so heavy.

3. Neutral Round (Shifting the Energy)

Eyebrow: Maybe it's okay to feel this way.

Side of Eye: I'm learning to manage it better.

Under Eye: I don't have to fix everything right now.

Under Nose: I'm allowed to take small steps.

Chin: What if this could get easier?

Collarbone: I'm open to finding peace.

Under Arm: I give myself space to breathe.

Top of Head: I am supporting myself in this moment.

4.   Positive Round (Reframe and Empower)

Eyebrow: I choose to feel calm and confident.

Side of Eye: I am capable of handling this.

Under Eye: I trust my process.

Under Nose: I honor my growth.

Chin: I am stronger than this challenge.

Collarbone: I am finding clarity and peace.

Under Arm: I am stepping into my power.

Top of Head: I deeply and completely love and accept myself.

11. TAPPING FOR PROCRASTINATION

1.   Karate Chop Point (Setup)

Even though I'm dealing with [issue], I deeply and completely love and accept myself.

Even though it feels overwhelming, I honor how I feel and am open to change.

Even though this [issue] is affecting my peace, I allow myself to let go and trust the process.

2.   Negative Round (Acknowledge the Issue)

Eyebrow: This [issue] is really getting to me.

Side of Eye: I feel so caught up in it.

Under Eye: It's draining my energy and focus.

Under Nose: I don't know how to handle it.

Chin: It's always there in the back of my mind.

Collarbone: I'm tired of this stress.

Under Arm: I just want relief.

Top of Head: This pressure feels so heavy.

3.   Neutral Round (Shifting the Energy)

Eyebrow: Maybe it's okay to feel this way.

Side of Eye: I'm learning to manage it better.

Under Eye: I don't have to fix everything right now.

Under Nose: I'm allowed to take small steps.

Chin: What if this could get easier?

Collarbone: I'm open to finding peace.

Under Arm: I give myself space to breathe.

Top of Head: I am supporting myself in this moment.

4. Positive Round (Reframe and Empower)

Eyebrow: I choose to feel calm and confident.

Side of Eye: I am capable of handling this.

Under Eye: I trust my process.

Under Nose: I honor my growth.

Chin: I am stronger than this challenge.

Collarbone: I am finding clarity and peace.

Under Arm: I am stepping into my power.

Top of Head: I deeply and completely love and accept myself.

12. TAPPING FOR DISTRACTION AND LACK OF FOCUS

1.   Karate Chop Point (Setup)

Even though I'm dealing with [issue], I deeply and completely love and accept myself.

Even though it feels overwhelming, I honor how I feel and am open to change.

Even though this [issue] is affecting my peace, I allow myself to let go and trust the process.

2. Negative Round (Acknowledge the Issue)

Eyebrow: This [issue] is really getting to me.

Side of Eye: I feel so caught up in it.

Under Eye: It's draining my energy and focus.

Under Nose: I don't know how to handle it.

Chin: It's always there in the back of my mind.

Collarbone: I'm tired of this stress.

Under Arm: I just want relief.

Top of Head: This pressure feels so heavy.

3.   Neutral Round (Shifting the Energy)

Eyebrow: Maybe it's okay to feel this way.

Side of Eye: I'm learning to manage it better.

Under Eye: I don't have to fix everything right now.

Under Nose: I'm allowed to take small steps.

Chin: What if this could get easier?

Collarbone: I'm open to finding peace.

Under Arm: I give myself space to breathe.

Top of Head: I am supporting myself in this moment.

4.   Positive Round (Reframe and Empower)

Eyebrow: I choose to feel calm and confident.

Side of Eye: I am capable of handling this.

Under Eye: I trust my process.

Under Nose: I honor my growth.

Chin: I am stronger than this challenge.

Collarbone: I am finding clarity and peace.

Under Arm: I am stepping into my power.

Top of Head: I deeply and completely love and accept myself.

13. TAPPING FOR CREATIVE BLOCK

1.   Karate Chop Point (Setup)

Even though I'm dealing with [issue], I deeply and completely love and accept myself.

Even though it feels overwhelming, I honor how I feel and am open to change.

Even though this [issue] is affecting my peace, I allow myself to let go and trust the process.

2.   Negative Round (Acknowledge the Issue)

Eyebrow: This [issue] is really getting to me.

Side of Eye: I feel so caught up in it.

Under Eye: It's draining my energy and focus.

Under Nose: I don't know how to handle it.

Chin: It's always there in the back of my mind.

Collarbone: I'm tired of this stress.

Under Arm: I just want relief.

Top of Head: This pressure feels so heavy.

3.   Neutral Round (Shifting the Energy)

Eyebrow: Maybe it's okay to feel this way.

Side of Eye: I'm learning to manage it better.

Under Eye: I don't have to fix everything right now.

Under Nose: I'm allowed to take small steps.

Chin: What if this could get easier?

Collarbone: I'm open to finding peace.

Under Arm: I give myself space to breathe.

Top of Head: I am supporting myself in this moment.

4.   Positive Round (Reframe and Empower)

Eyebrow: I choose to feel calm and confident.

Side of Eye: I am capable of handling this.

Under Eye: I trust my process.

Under Nose: I honor my growth.

Chin: I am stronger than this challenge.

Collarbone: I am finding clarity and peace.

Under Arm: I am stepping into my power.

Top of Head: I deeply and completely love and accept myself.

14. TAPPING FOR DREAD BEFORE PRESENTATIONS OR MEETINGS

1. Karate Chop Point (Setup)

Even though I'm dealing with [issue], I deeply and completely love and accept myself.

Even though it feels overwhelming, I honor how I feel and am open to change.

Even though this [issue] is affecting my peace, I allow myself to let go and trust the process.

2. Negative Round (Acknowledge the Issue)

Eyebrow: This [issue] is really getting to me.

Side of Eye: I feel so caught up in it.

Under Eye: It's draining my energy and focus.

Under Nose: I don't know how to handle it.

Chin: It's always there in the back of my mind.

Collarbone: I'm tired of this stress.

Under Arm: I just want relief.

Top of Head: This pressure feels so heavy.

3. Neutral Round (Shifting the Energy)

Eyebrow: Maybe it's okay to feel this way.

Side of Eye: I'm learning to manage it better.

Under Eye: I don't have to fix everything right now.

Under Nose: I'm allowed to take small steps.

Chin: What if this could get easier?

Collarbone: I'm open to finding peace.

Under Arm: I give myself space to breathe.

Top of Head: I am supporting myself in this moment.

4. Positive Round (Reframe and Empower)

Eyebrow: I choose to feel calm and confident.

Side of Eye: I am capable of handling this.

Under Eye: I trust my process.

Under Nose: I honor my growth.

Chin: I am stronger than this challenge.

Collarbone: I am finding clarity and peace.

Under Arm: I am stepping into my power.

Top of Head: I deeply and completely love and accept myself.

15. TAPPING FOR FINISHING WHAT YOU START

1.   Karate Chop Point (Setup)

Even though I'm dealing with [issue], I deeply and completely love and accept myself.

Even though it feels overwhelming, I honor how I feel and am open to change.

Even though this [issue] is affecting my peace, I allow myself to let go and trust the process.

2.   Negative Round (Acknowledge the Issue)

Eyebrow: This [issue] is really getting to me.

Side of Eye: I feel so caught up in it.

Under Eye: It's draining my energy and focus.

Under Nose: I don't know how to handle it.

Chin: It's always there in the back of my mind.

Collarbone: I'm tired of this stress.

Under Arm: I just want relief.

Top of Head: This pressure feels so heavy.

3.   Neutral Round (Shifting the Energy)

Eyebrow: Maybe it's okay to feel this way.

Side of Eye: I'm learning to manage it better.

Under Eye: I don't have to fix everything right now.

Under Nose: I'm allowed to take small steps.

Chin: What if this could get easier?

Collarbone: I'm open to finding peace.

Under Arm: I give myself space to breathe.

Top of Head: I am supporting myself in this moment.

4.   Positive Round (Reframe and Empower)

Eyebrow: I choose to feel calm and confident.

Side of Eye: I am capable of handling this.

Under Eye: I trust my process.

Under Nose: I honor my growth.

Chin: I am stronger than this challenge.

Collarbone: I am finding clarity and peace.

Under Arm: I am stepping into my power.

Top of Head: I deeply and completely love and accept myself.

16. TAPPING FOR GUILT AROUND TAKING BREAKS

1.   Karate Chop Point (Setup)

Even though I'm dealing with [issue], I deeply and completely love and accept myself.

Even though it feels overwhelming, I honor how I feel and am open to change.

Even though this [issue] is affecting my peace, I allow myself to let go and trust the process.

2.   Negative Round (Acknowledge the Issue)

Eyebrow: This [issue] is really getting to me.

Side of Eye: I feel so caught up in it.

Under Eye: It's draining my energy and focus.

Under Nose: I don't know how to handle it.

Chin: It's always there in the back of my mind.

Collarbone: I'm tired of this stress.

Under Arm: I just want relief.

Top of Head: This pressure feels so heavy.

3.   Neutral Round (Shifting the Energy)

Eyebrow: Maybe it's okay to feel this way.

Side of Eye: I'm learning to manage it better.

Under Eye: I don't have to fix everything right now.

Under Nose: I'm allowed to take small steps.

Chin: What if this could get easier?

Collarbone: I'm open to finding peace.

Under Arm: I give myself space to breathe.

Top of Head: I am supporting myself in this moment.

4.   Positive Round (Reframe and Empower)

Eyebrow: I choose to feel calm and confident.

Side of Eye: I am capable of handling this.

Under Eye: I trust my process.

Under Nose: I honor my growth.

Chin: I am stronger than this challenge.

Collarbone: I am finding clarity and peace.

Under Arm: I am stepping into my power.

Top of Head: I deeply and completely love and accept myself.

17. TAPPING FOR WORK-LIFE BALANCE

1.   Karate Chop Point (Setup)

Even though I'm dealing with [issue], I deeply and completely love and accept myself.

Even though it feels overwhelming, I honor how I feel and am open to change.

Even though this [issue] is affecting my peace, I allow myself to let go and trust the process.

2.   Negative Round (Acknowledge the Issue)

Eyebrow: This [issue] is really getting to me.

Side of Eye: I feel so caught up in it.

Under Eye: It's draining my energy and focus.

Under Nose: I don't know how to handle it.

Chin: It's always there in the back of my mind.

Collarbone: I'm tired of this stress.

Under Arm: I just want relief.

Top of Head: This pressure feels so heavy.

3.   Neutral Round (Shifting the Energy)

Eyebrow: Maybe it's okay to feel this way.

Side of Eye: I'm learning to manage it better.

Under Eye: I don't have to fix everything right now.

Under Nose: I'm allowed to take small steps.

Chin: What if this could get easier?

Collarbone: I'm open to finding peace.

Under Arm: I give myself space to breathe.

Top of Head: I am supporting myself in this moment.

4. Positive Round (Reframe and Empower)

Eyebrow: I choose to feel calm and confident.

Side of Eye: I am capable of handling this.

Under Eye: I trust my process.

Under Nose: I honor my growth.

Chin: I am stronger than this challenge.

Collarbone: I am finding clarity and peace.

Under Arm: I am stepping into my power.

Top of Head: I deeply and completely love and accept myself.

18. TAPPING FOR BURNOUT RECOVERY

1.   Karate Chop Point (Setup)

Even though I'm dealing with [issue], I deeply and completely love and accept myself.

Even though it feels overwhelming, I honor how I feel and am open to change.

Even though this [issue] is affecting my peace, I allow myself to let go and trust the process.

2.   Negative Round (Acknowledge the Issue)

Eyebrow: This [issue] is really getting to me.

Side of Eye: I feel so caught up in it.

Under Eye: It's draining my energy and focus.

Under Nose: I don't know how to handle it.

Chin: It's always there in the back of my mind.

Collarbone: I'm tired of this stress.

Under Arm: I just want relief.

Top of Head: This pressure feels so heavy.

3.   Neutral Round (Shifting the Energy)

Eyebrow: Maybe it's okay to feel this way.

Side of Eye: I'm learning to manage it better.

Under Eye: I don't have to fix everything right now.

Under Nose: I'm allowed to take small steps.

Chin: What if this could get easier?

Collarbone: I'm open to finding peace.

Under Arm: I give myself space to breathe.

Top of Head: I am supporting myself in this moment.

4.　Positive Round (Reframe and Empower)

Eyebrow: I choose to feel calm and confident.

Side of Eye: I am capable of handling this.

Under Eye: I trust my process.

Under Nose: I honor my growth.

Chin: I am stronger than this challenge.

Collarbone: I am finding clarity and peace.

Under Arm: I am stepping into my power.

Top of Head: I deeply and completely love and accept myself.

19. TAPPING FOR SAYING "NO" AND SETTING BOUNDARIES

1.   Karate Chop Point (Setup)

Even though I'm dealing with [issue], I deeply and completely love and accept myself.

Even though it feels overwhelming, I honor how I feel and am open to change.

Even though this [issue] is affecting my peace, I allow myself to let go and trust the process.

2.   Negative Round (Acknowledge the Issue)

Eyebrow: This [issue] is really getting to me.

Side of Eye: I feel so caught up in it.

Under Eye: It's draining my energy and focus.

Under Nose: I don't know how to handle it.

Chin: It's always there in the back of my mind.

Collarbone: I'm tired of this stress.

Under Arm: I just want relief.

Top of Head: This pressure feels so heavy.

3.   Neutral Round (Shifting the Energy)

Eyebrow: Maybe it's okay to feel this way.

Side of Eye: I'm learning to manage it better.

Under Eye: I don't have to fix everything right now.

Under Nose: I'm allowed to take small steps.

Chin: What if this could get easier?

Collarbone: I'm open to finding peace.

Under Arm: I give myself space to breathe.

Top of Head: I am supporting myself in this moment.

4.   Positive Round (Reframe and Empower)

Eyebrow: I choose to feel calm and confident.

Side of Eye: I am capable of handling this.

Under Eye: I trust my process.

Under Nose: I honor my growth.

Chin: I am stronger than this challenge.

Collarbone: I am finding clarity and peace.

Under Arm: I am stepping into my power.

Top of Head: I deeply and completely love and accept myself.

20. TAPPING FOR SLEEP TROUBLES FROM WORK STRESS

1.   Karate Chop Point (Setup)

Even though I'm dealing with [issue], I deeply and completely love and accept myself.

Even though it feels overwhelming, I honor how I feel and am open to change.

Even though this [issue] is affecting my peace, I allow myself to let go and trust the process.

2.   Negative Round (Acknowledge the Issue)

Eyebrow: This [issue] is really getting to me.

Side of Eye: I feel so caught up in it.

Under Eye: It's draining my energy and focus.

Under Nose: I don't know how to handle it.

Chin: It's always there in the back of my mind.

Collarbone: I'm tired of this stress.

Under Arm: I just want relief.

Top of Head: This pressure feels so heavy.

3.   Neutral Round (Shifting the Energy)

Eyebrow: Maybe it's okay to feel this way.

Side of Eye: I'm learning to manage it better.

Under Eye: I don't have to fix everything right now.

Under Nose: I'm allowed to take small steps.

Chin: What if this could get easier?

Collarbone: I'm open to finding peace.

Under Arm: I give myself space to breathe.

Top of Head: I am supporting myself in this moment.

4.   Positive Round (Reframe and Empower)

Eyebrow: I choose to feel calm and confident.

Side of Eye: I am capable of handling this.

Under Eye: I trust my process.

Under Nose: I honor my growth.

Chin: I am stronger than this challenge.

Collarbone: I am finding clarity and peace.

Under Arm: I am stepping into my power.

Top of Head: I deeply and completely love and accept myself.

21. TAPPING FOR TOXIC COLLEAGUE DYNAMICS

1.   Karate Chop Point (Setup)

Even though I'm dealing with [issue], I deeply and completely love and accept myself.

Even though it feels overwhelming, I honor how I feel and am open to change.

Even though this [issue] is affecting my peace, I allow myself to let go and trust the process.

2.   Negative Round (Acknowledge the Issue)

Eyebrow: This [issue] is really getting to me.

Side of Eye: I feel so caught up in it.

Under Eye: It's draining my energy and focus.

Under Nose: I don't know how to handle it.

Chin: It's always there in the back of my mind.

Collarbone: I'm tired of this stress.

Under Arm: I just want relief.

Top of Head: This pressure feels so heavy.

3.   Neutral Round (Shifting the Energy)

Eyebrow: Maybe it's okay to feel this way.

Side of Eye: I'm learning to manage it better.

Under Eye: I don't have to fix everything right now.

Under Nose: I'm allowed to take small steps.

Chin: What if this could get easier?

Collarbone: I'm open to finding peace.

Under Arm: I give myself space to breathe.

Top of Head: I am supporting myself in this moment.

4.   Positive Round (Reframe and Empower)

Eyebrow: I choose to feel calm and confident.

Side of Eye: I am capable of handling this.

Under Eye: I trust my process.

Under Nose: I honor my growth.

Chin: I am stronger than this challenge.

Collarbone: I am finding clarity and peace.

Under Arm: I am stepping into my power.

Top of Head: I deeply and completely love and accept myself.

22. TAPPING FOR CONFLICT WITH A BOSS OR CLIENT

1. Karate Chop Point (Setup)

Even though I'm dealing with [issue], I deeply and completely love and accept myself.

Even though it feels overwhelming, I honor how I feel and am open to change.

Even though this [issue] is affecting my peace, I allow myself to let go and trust the process.

2. Negative Round (Acknowledge the Issue)

Eyebrow: This [issue] is really getting to me.

Side of Eye: I feel so caught up in it.

Under Eye: It's draining my energy and focus.

Under Nose: I don't know how to handle it.

Chin: It's always there in the back of my mind.

Collarbone: I'm tired of this stress.

Under Arm: I just want relief.

Top of Head: This pressure feels so heavy.

3. Neutral Round (Shifting the Energy)

Eyebrow: Maybe it's okay to feel this way.

Side of Eye: I'm learning to manage it better.

Under Eye: I don't have to fix everything right now.

Under Nose: I'm allowed to take small steps.

Chin: What if this could get easier?

Collarbone: I'm open to finding peace.

Under Arm: I give myself space to breathe.

Top of Head: I am supporting myself in this moment.

4.   Positive Round (Reframe and Empower)

Eyebrow: I choose to feel calm and confident.

Side of Eye: I am capable of handling this.

Under Eye: I trust my process.

Under Nose: I honor my growth.

Chin: I am stronger than this challenge.

Collarbone: I am finding clarity and peace.

Under Arm: I am stepping into my power.

Top of Head: I deeply and completely love and accept myself.

23. TAPPING FOR BEING UNDERVALUED OR UNAPPRECIATED

1.   Karate Chop Point (Setup)

Even though I'm dealing with [issue], I deeply and completely love and accept myself.

Even though it feels overwhelming, I honor how I feel and am open to change.

Even though this [issue] is affecting my peace, I allow myself to let go and trust the process.

2.   Negative Round (Acknowledge the Issue)

Eyebrow: This [issue] is really getting to me.

Side of Eye: I feel so caught up in it.

Under Eye: It's draining my energy and focus.

Under Nose: I don't know how to handle it.

Chin: It's always there in the back of my mind.

Collarbone: I'm tired of this stress.

Under Arm: I just want relief.

Top of Head: This pressure feels so heavy.

3.   Neutral Round (Shifting the Energy)

Eyebrow: Maybe it's okay to feel this way.

Side of Eye: I'm learning to manage it better.

Under Eye: I don't have to fix everything right now.

Under Nose: I'm allowed to take small steps.

Chin: What if this could get easier?

Collarbone: I'm open to finding peace.

Under Arm: I give myself space to breathe.

Top of Head: I am supporting myself in this moment.

4.   Positive Round (Reframe and Empower)

Eyebrow: I choose to feel calm and confident.

Side of Eye: I am capable of handling this.

Under Eye: I trust my process.

Under Nose: I honor my growth.

Chin: I am stronger than this challenge.

Collarbone: I am finding clarity and peace.

Under Arm: I am stepping into my power.

Top of Head: I deeply and completely love and accept myself.

24. TAPPING FOR EMOTIONAL DETACHMENT AT WORK

1.   Karate Chop Point (Setup)

Even though I'm dealing with [issue], I deeply and completely love and accept myself.

Even though it feels overwhelming, I honor how I feel and am open to change.

Even though this [issue] is affecting my peace, I allow myself to let go and trust the process.

2.   Negative Round (Acknowledge the Issue)

Eyebrow: This [issue] is really getting to me.

Side of Eye: I feel so caught up in it.

Under Eye: It's draining my energy and focus.

Under Nose: I don't know how to handle it.

Chin: It's always there in the back of my mind.

Collarbone: I'm tired of this stress.

Under Arm: I just want relief.

Top of Head: This pressure feels so heavy.

3.   Neutral Round (Shifting the Energy)

Eyebrow: Maybe it's okay to feel this way.

Side of Eye: I'm learning to manage it better.

Under Eye: I don't have to fix everything right now.

Under Nose: I'm allowed to take small steps.

Chin: What if this could get easier?

Collarbone: I'm open to finding peace.

Under Arm: I give myself space to breathe.

Top of Head: I am supporting myself in this moment.

4.   Positive Round (Reframe and Empower)

Eyebrow: I choose to feel calm and confident.

Side of Eye: I am capable of handling this.

Under Eye: I trust my process.

Under Nose: I honor my growth.

Chin: I am stronger than this challenge.

Collarbone: I am finding clarity and peace.

Under Arm: I am stepping into my power.

Top of Head: I deeply and completely love and accept myself.

25. TAPPING FOR RELEASING WORKDAY NEGATIVITY BEFORE GOING HOME

1.   Karate Chop Point (Setup)

Even though I'm dealing with [issue], I deeply and completely love and accept myself.

Even though it feels overwhelming, I honor how I feel and am open to change.

Even though this [issue] is affecting my peace, I allow myself to let go and trust the process.

2.   Negative Round (Acknowledge the Issue)

Eyebrow: This [issue] is really getting to me.

Side of Eye: I feel so caught up in it.

Under Eye: It's draining my energy and focus.

Under Nose: I don't know how to handle it.

Chin: It's always there in the back of my mind.

Collarbone: I'm tired of this stress.

Under Arm: I just want relief.

Top of Head: This pressure feels so heavy.

3.   Neutral Round (Shifting the Energy)

Eyebrow: Maybe it's okay to feel this way.

Side of Eye: I'm learning to manage it better.

Under Eye: I don't have to fix everything right now.

Under Nose: I'm allowed to take small steps.

Chin: What if this could get easier?

Collarbone: I'm open to finding peace.

Under Arm: I give myself space to breathe.

Top of Head: I am supporting myself in this moment.

4.   Positive Round (Reframe and Empower)

Eyebrow: I choose to feel calm and confident.

Side of Eye: I am capable of hanWdling this.

Under Eye: I trust my process.

Under Nose: I honor my growth.

Chin: I am stronger than this challenge.

Collarbone: I am finding clarity and peace.

Under Arm: I am stepping into my power.

Top of Head: I deeply and completely love and accept myself.

Chapter 13

Rewire & Rise - 15 DIY NLP Hacks to Master the Corporate Mind

In today's high-pressure work environments, NLP (Neuro-Linguistic Programming) offers powerful self-coaching tools to rewire limiting beliefs, increase emotional resilience, and unlock high performance. Below are 15 step-by-step NLP practices working professionals can apply anytime, anywhere.

1.   The Confidence Anchor

- Recall a moment when you felt incredibly confident.

- Close your eyes and relive that memory in vivid detail: sights, sounds, feelings.

- As you relive the peak moment, squeeze your thumb and forefinger together.

- Repeat daily with different empowering memories to reinforce the anchor.

- Use the same gesture (thumb-finger squeeze) before important events to activate confidence.

2.   The Reframe Technique

- Identify a stressful or negative situation.

- Write down the current belief or interpretation (e.g., 'My boss micromanages me because they don't trust me.').

- Now ask: What else could this mean? Try 2–3 alternative positive or neutral interpretations.

- Choose the interpretation that empowers you most and consciously adopt it.

- Revisit the reframe when the situation arises again.

3.   Swish Pattern for Overthinking

- Visualize the negative thought/image that causes stress or overthinking.

- Now create a contrasting, positive image of how you want to feel/act.

- Place the negative image in your mental foreground and the positive one in the background.

- Quickly 'swish'—make the negative image shrink and fade while the positive image becomes large and bright.

- Repeat 5–7 times until the negative image loses its emotional charge.

4.   Future Self Dialogue

- Find a quiet place to sit and close your eyes.

- Visualize your ideal future self 5–10 years from now—confident, fulfilled, successful.

- Ask your future self questions: What helped you get here? What would you do in my current situation?

- Listen to the answers intuitively and journal them afterward.

- Take one aligned action that your future self advised.

5.   Chunking Down

- Choose a task that feels overwhelming.

- Ask: What is the first small step I can take toward completing this?

- Break it down further: What would that look like in 10 minutes?

- Write down each step on paper and tick them off as you go.

- Use this approach consistently to build momentum and reduce anxiety.

6.   Visual Squash for Internal Conflict

- Identify two conflicting desires or thoughts (e.g., 'I want to relax' vs. 'I should work late').

- Hold out both hands as if each hand holds one part.

- Visualize each desire in your hands and observe their intention.

- Bring your hands slowly together, imagining the two parts uniting into a balanced whole.

- Bring your hands to your heart and breathe deeply, affirming the integration.

7. The Movie Recode Technique

- Replay a stressful memory in your mind like a movie.

- Now imagine rewinding it in fast motion and shrinking the image.

- Add funny music or colors to lighten the mood of the memory.

- Replay the new version and notice how the emotional charge decreases.

- Practice this to neutralize past negative workplace memories.

8. Circle of Excellence

- Stand and visualize a circle in front of you on the floor filled with radiant light.

- Imagine your most empowered self standing in the circle—confident, clear, composed.

- Step into the circle and feel the energy, posture, and mindset of that version of you.

- Breathe in the confidence and anchor that state.

- Step out and re-enter the circle anytime you need a boost at work.

9. Meta Mirror for Conflict Resolution

- Visualize yourself and the person you're in conflict with sitting opposite you.

- Now imagine switching roles—step into their shoes and understand their perspective.

- Switch back and reflect on how this changes your understanding.

- Find a new, empathetic approach to respond to the conflict.

- Use this before difficult conversations for greater emotional intelligence.

10.   Anchoring a Calm State

- Recall a time you felt deeply relaxed and calm.

- Relive the moment in full sensory detail (what did you see, hear, feel?).

- At the peak of the calm feeling, press your knuckles or wrist.

- Repeat daily with the same pressure and memory.

- Use the anchored gesture before meetings or stressful tasks to stay composed.

11.   Belief Change with Affirmation Looping

- Identify a limiting belief (e.g., 'I don't deserve success').

- Replace it with a positive belief ('I am worthy of success').

- Repeat the new belief slowly, in front of a mirror, looking into your eyes.

- Feel the belief settling in as you speak.

- Do this twice daily for 21 days to rewire your inner dialogue.

12.   Time Line Therapy Lite

- Close your eyes and visualize a mental timeline of your life.

- Float above the timeline and move to the past moment you want to heal.

- Imagine sending light and healing to that moment.

- Now return to the present and imagine a bright, empowered future.

- Do this weekly to resolve emotional baggage.

13.   Mirror Motivation

- Stand in front of a mirror and make eye contact with yourself.

- Say your goal aloud followed by a power phrase (e.g., 'I will crush this deadline. I've got this!').

- Repeat it with increasing intensity and smile confidently.

- Repeat daily before leaving for work or starting a project.

14.   Pattern Interrupt Ritual

- When you feel a negative spiral coming (stress, overthinking), stand up immediately.

- Clap your hands loudly or do a quick shake-off with your body.

- Say an interrupting phrase like 'Reset. Refresh. Refocus.'

- Take a deep breath and resume with fresh energy.

15. Daily Intent Mapping

- Each morning, write down 3 intentions for your day (e.g., stay calm in meetings, appreciate your team, complete one key task).

- Visualize yourself achieving them smoothly and easily.

- End your day by reviewing what you accomplished and celebrating small wins.

Chapter 14

Mind Code – 13 Hypnoheal Journeys to Unlock Career Calm & Clarity

Before you begin your journey through the Hypnoheal scripts, it's essential to understand how to prepare your mind and body for deep, effective transformation. Hypnohealing relies on the principle that our subconscious mind—when relaxed and receptive—can absorb new beliefs, heal emotional wounds, and unlock our hidden potential.

This introduction will guide you through the steps of entering a relaxed, meditative state so that each visualization you experience becomes a powerful act of self-healing and transformation.

Step 1: Find a Quiet, Comfortable Space

Choose a space where you won't be disturbed for at least 10–15 minutes. Sit in a chair with your back straight or lie down with your arms resting gently at your sides. Keep your environment dimly lit or softly lit, and silence all distractions—phones, notifications, etc.

Step 2: Focus on Your Breath

Close your eyes. Begin by taking slow, deep breaths—inhaling for a count of four, holding for a count of four, and exhaling for a count of four. Repeat this for a few minutes until your body starts to relax.

Step 3: Progressive Muscle Relaxation

Gently scan your body from head to toe. As you mentally travel through each part, consciously relax that area. Release tension from your forehead, your jaw, your shoulders, your chest, your arms, your legs. With each breath, imagine the stress melting away.

Step 4: Visualization – Entering the Hypnotic State

Now, visualize yourself walking down a beautiful staircase. With each step down, you feel heavier, more relaxed, and safe. Count each step as you descend from 10 to 1. At the bottom, visualize a peaceful place—a garden, a beach, a forest—whatever feels safe and soothing.

Step 5: Affirm Safety and Openness

In this deeply relaxed state, say to yourself: "I am safe. I am open to healing. I allow my subconscious to guide me." These affirmations set the stage for deeper work.

Step 6: Begin the Script

Now that you're in a receptive mental space, begin the Hypnoheal script of your choice. Read it in your mind slowly or have someone guide you through it in a gentle voice. You may also record the script in your own voice and play it back during your practice.

Step 7: Grounding Back into Awareness

When the script ends, count slowly from 1 to 5 and tell yourself: "I am coming back refreshed, relaxed, and empowered." Wiggle your fingers and toes, open your eyes, and drink some water to ground yourself.

Hypnohealing is most effective when practiced consistently. Try one script daily or alternate based on your needs. With time, these visualizations will create deep, lasting shifts in your mind, behavior, and energy.

Now, let your healing journey begin.

HypnoHeal Scripts for enhancing performance at work

1.   Confidence Amplifier

- Find a quiet space where you can sit comfortably.

- Close your eyes and take three deep breaths, each one deeper than the last.

- Imagine a soft golden light forming around you, warm and energizing.

- Visualize yourself standing on a stage. The lights are on, the audience is silent and attentive.

- Feel your heart beat with excitement and confidence.

- Hear yourself speaking with clarity, conviction, and ease.

- The audience applauds as you finish—you smile, proud and empowered.

- Take this feeling into your day. You are ready. You are powerful.

2.   Morning Motivation Reset

- Lie down or sit in a quiet place with your back straight.

- Close your eyes and inhale deeply, imagining golden sunlight filling your lungs.

- Exhale all doubts and tension.

- Visualize yourself waking up on the perfect morning, full of purpose and clarity.

- See yourself moving through your day with ease, checking off tasks joyfully.

- Repeat mentally: 'Today is a fresh start. I am focused and ready.'

- Slowly bring awareness back to your body, and open your eyes with a smile.

3. Anxiety Release at Work

- Sit back and place your feet flat on the ground. Close your eyes.

- Take five deep, calming breaths.

- Imagine rising above your workspace in a gentle balloon.

- From this view, everything below looks smaller and less urgent.

- Let a breeze of peace wash over you. Feel your shoulders drop and mind clear.

- Repeat mentally: 'I choose calm. I breathe through pressure.'

- Float gently back down and open your eyes when you're ready.

4. Decision-Making Clarity

- Sit quietly, spine straight, hands resting gently.

- Close your eyes and breathe deeply, relaxing with every exhale.

- Visualize walking down a hallway with three glowing doors ahead of you.

- Each door represents a choice. Stand before each and feel what your body tells you.

- Open the door that feels most right—step inside.

- See your future self, successful, at peace, thriving.

- Take a message from this space and slowly return to the present with that clarity.

5.　Fear of Public Speaking

- Close your eyes and visualize a calm ocean, steady waves relaxing your breath.

- Imagine standing on a stage. The spotlight is soft, warm.

- The audience is friendly, smiling, nodding in support.

- Hear your voice strong, clear, and powerful.

- Let this image imprint deeply—this is your truth.

- Repeat: 'My voice matters. I speak with calm confidence.'

- Bring this energy with you as you open your eyes.

6.   Burnout Recovery Oasis

- Find a quiet space. Close your eyes and imagine a lush forest.

- Walk along a path where sunlight streams through tall trees.

- A gentle stream flows beside you. Sit by it and dip your hands into the water.

- With each breath, absorb nature's strength. Release the weight of your workload.

- Feel renewed, restored, and whole.

- Visualize taking this peace into your workday.

- Open your eyes refreshed and empowered.

7.   Abundance Magnetizer

- Relax your body and breathe into your heart center.

- Visualize a radiant beam of light above your head pouring gold dust over you.

- Feel wealth, opportunity, and recognition flowing into your life.

- See emails, messages, or people coming to support your career.

- Repeat: 'I am worthy. I attract success effortlessly.'

- Anchor this feeling in your body before gently opening your eyes.

8.   Conflict Transformation

- Close your eyes and visualize a calm lake.

- Bring to mind a recent workplace conflict.

- Imagine the person involved sitting across the lake from you.

- Speak silently to them from your heart, then listen.

- Breathe in forgiveness and exhale the tension.

- See yourselves shaking hands, resolved and at peace.

- Let this image guide your next real-life interaction.

## 9.	Focus and Flow Booster

- Sit in a quiet space. Visualize a beam of light entering your forehead.

- This light brings deep concentration and clears mental fog.

- Picture yourself completing a task with ease and joy.

- Repeat: 'I am in flow. I accomplish with grace and focus.'

- When ready, open your eyes and begin your task with renewed clarity.

10.   Inner Critic Rewiring

- Close your eyes. Picture your inner critic as a shadow figure.

- Ask: 'Why do you speak this way?' Listen calmly.

- Now, imagine that figure transforming into a supportive mentor.

- Hear it say kind, motivating words.

- Repeat: 'I choose to believe in my growth.'

- Thank the new voice and gently return to your present moment.

11. Work-Life Balance Ritual

- Visualize a serene lake surrounded by trees at twilight.

- See one side representing work, the other family and self.

- Walk a path that evenly connects the two.

- Feel harmony in both spaces. Let go of guilt, reclaim your boundaries.

- Repeat: 'I honor both my ambition and my rest.'

- Inhale balance. Exhale overwhelm.

12. Promotion Visualization

- Close your eyes. See yourself entering your dream office.

- Notice the desk, the view, the smile on your face.

- Feel the pride, hear the congratulations, receive your new title.

- Repeat: 'I am prepared. I welcome this next level.'

- Open your eyes with determination and certainty.

13. Procrastination Breakthrough

- Close your eyes and visualize a large brick wall in front of you.

- This wall represents your delay and avoidance.

- Now, visualize yourself smashing through it or walking around it with ease.

- On the other side is your success—see yourself working with excitement.

- Repeat: 'I choose progress over perfection.'

- Open your eyes and take one immediate step forward.

Chapter 15

Conclusion - Coming Home to Wholeness

As we arrive at the final pages of this journey, let us pause and take a deep breath—not just to mark the end of a book, but to honor the beginning of something far more profound. This isn't merely a collection of chapters, techniques, or insights. It is a homecoming. A return to your truest, most aligned self—the self that's been waiting beneath the layers of deadlines, roles, and relentless pursuit of success.

In Chapter 1, we started with a shared reality—the corporate stress epidemic. We acknowledged the silent burnout that creeps through offices, boardrooms, and homes. We gave voice to the mental load carried by high performers, and we understood that the cost of chronic stress is not just organizational—it's deeply personal.

From there, Chapter 2 expanded our perspective. We uncovered that spirituality is not a luxury reserved for quiet monasteries or faraway retreats—it is the missing link in modern leadership. We saw how companies like Google, Apple, and mindful leaders worldwide have successfully embraced spiritual practices to foster clarity, empathy, and innovation. Spirituality, we learned, is the fuel that powers sustainable success.

Chapter 3 brought us into the gentle rhythm of Emotional Freedom Technique (EFT). With tapping sequences and affirmations, we began to release the invisible blocks held in our energy systems. From the anxious executive to the self-doubting manager, EFT reminded us that healing doesn't need to be complicated. It just needs to be practiced—with love, patience, and presence.

Chapter 4 took us deeper through the transformative world of Past Life Regression (PLR). We examined how the echoes of our past—whether real or metaphorical—shape the stories we live today. By accessing those imprints through regression, we free ourselves from subconscious narratives and open the path for purposeful living.

Chapter 5 asked us to turn inward and meet our shadow. Shadow Work Healing revealed that our greatest obstacles are often not in the external world but in the unacknowledged parts of ourselves. Through courageous self-inquiry, we found buried strengths in our insecurities, empathy in our anger, and wisdom in our fears.

Chapter 6 introduced the power of Hypnohealing, where we met the subconscious mind—the silent architect of our beliefs, behaviors, and dreams. With self-hypnosis and deep relaxation, we gently rewired the limiting beliefs that had kept us stuck and replaced them with new truths that align with our soul's potential.

Then came Chapter 7—Tarot Life Coaching. Here, we rediscovered the forgotten language of symbols and intuition. We moved beyond rigid thinking into a space where inner knowing leads. Tarot became less about prediction and more about reflection. It taught us to ask better questions, seek deeper truths, and trust the unseen currents that shape our decisions.

Chapter 8 unfolded the realm of NLP—Neuro-Linguistic Programming—where words became tools for transformation. We learned how language, imagery, and behavioral patterning can reshape our inner and outer worlds. NLP gave us structured practices to reprogram fear, boost confidence, and step into roles of authentic leadership.

Chapter 9 integrated it all. It showed us how these modalities can become living practices in the corporate landscape. We reimagined workspaces as places not just of profit, but of purpose. We envisioned meditation rooms instead of burnout clinics, intuitive coaching over mechanical evaluations, and wellness retreats in place of punitive appraisals.

And then came Chapter 10—The Blueprint. A step-by-step plan for working professionals to not just cope, but to thrive. From morning rituals to weekly resets, we offered a schedule that supports performance, well-being, and emotional intelligence. It was a roadmap for those who are ready to lead their lives—and their teams—consciously.

And finally, Chapter 11 invited us to dream bigger. It was about the organizational shift. The vision of a spiritually conscious workplace where policies reflect compassion, where meetings begin with mindfulness, where mentorship includes healing, and where KPIs measure not just output but emotional engagement.

Next came the DIY scripts of the methodologies that are effective in bringing about deep transformations if practiced thoughtfully and thoroughly.

Dear reader, this book is not the end. It's a toolkit, a lighthouse, a gentle reminder that you are not broken—you are awakening.

You are not behind—you are right on time.

You don't need to climb harder—you need to align deeper.

Let this be the moment you choose to show up for yourself, not with force, but with grace. Let this be the season you lead with intuition, you heal with humility, and you succeed with soul.

Carry these practices into your boardrooms and brainstorming sessions. Speak about them at your dinner tables. Normalize conversations about energy, emotions, and intuition. Be the bridge between performance and purpose, between strategy and spirit.

And remember—no matter how demanding your job, how loud the world, or how uncertain the road may seem, the tools are now in your hands. Tap into them. Journal with them. Breathe with them. Let them hold you when you falter and lift you when you rise.

You are not alone. You are not too late. You are not too much.

You are exactly who you need to be—and this journey has only just begun.

Thank you for taking this path with me. I believe in your transformation, and I celebrate the light that you will carry into this world.

With love, belief, and alignment,

Paromita Banerjee Sarkar

About the Author

Paromita Banerjee Sarkar is a woman on a mission—one that is deeply rooted in her passion for helping others lead happier, more fulfilling lives. At the core of her being is an unwavering commitment to removing stress, anxiety, and unnecessary burdens that prevent people from realizing their true potential. She is a natural communicator, an insightful storyteller, and a compassionate listener, making her a guiding force in the world of personal excellence and transformation.

With over two decades of experience across prestigious corporate giants like the Tata Group, Reliance Jio, Aditya Birla Group, and Accenture, Paromita has carved an extraordinary path at the intersection of high-performance management and holistic wellness. Her professional credentials are both impressive and multifaceted—ranging from senior leadership roles in product management, marketing strategy, and business consulting to profound expertise in Emotional Freedom Technique (EFT), NLP, Past Life Regression, Shadow Work, Tarot Life Coaching, and Hypnohealing.

Paromita's journey is not just one of corporate success, but of deep spiritual evolution. She blends the analytical acumen of a strategist with the intuitive wisdom of a healer. This unique integration makes her teachings especially impactful for working professionals seeking not just to survive in high-pressure environments, but to thrive with clarity, joy, and purpose.

Her philosophy is rooted in three transformative themes: Spirituality & Personal Excellence, Communication & Storytelling, and a Performance-Oriented Mindset. These principles form the foundation of her life's work and the core of her methodology. Whether she's conducting workshops, coaching individuals, or speaking at conferences, Paromita empowers people to realign with their inner truth, build emotional resilience, and unlock their highest potential.

As the founder of "Timeless Soul Healings," Paromita is creating a legacy—one that brings ancient healing wisdom into the modern workplace. She believes that organizations can be both profitable and compassionate, that success can coexist with soul, and that true transformation begins from within.

Through her writing, teachings, and healing programs, Paromita continues to inspire a new generation of conscious leaders who are ready to bring heart, harmony, and higher purpose into the corporate world and beyond.

Write to us: timelesssoulhealings@gmail.com

Connect @ www.linkedin.com/in/paromitabanerjeesarkar